The Sound of the Tang Dynasty

悠远唐音

English Poems that Sprang from the Chinese Original

Great poetry is an artistic creation with the best of the human mind and heart working together. If poetry only has heart, something is missing. Nor can poetry be complete if it is only the mind at work with many abstractions. Of course we cannot enter the minds and hearts from which great poetry comes but through this poetry we savor the intellectual vigor and emotional strength of the poet. The best poetry at times presents creation or the physical world in all its splendor or atrocity. Other times, it is the unique person or the human characteristics we all share that stands forth in the poem.

The Tang dynasty was a time of great poets and poetry. Rare is the Chinese person, today or in history, who cannot recite lines from Tang poems and whose life has not been influenced by the words of great poets such as Wang Wei, Li Bai, or Tu Fu. Indeed, the Chinese often see the world and others through the eyes of these poets.

This collection of Tang dynasty poems, so carefully prepared by Michael Dong Botao, gives us a chance, once again to interact with both the mundane and ineffable as expressed by these poems, often with just a few lines of Chinese characters – the brevity of which in no way suggests the lack of profoundness. This book is not to be rushed through; a poem or two a day is enough to make the day infinitely richer.

What is special about this collection is that there is not only the Chinese original text of the poem, and a version of the poem expressed in modern Chinese, but there is also a thoughtful interpretation of the poem revealing how much time the editor has spent pondering on how to read and understand the poem. Beside all these elements, there is also an English version of the Chinese poem, which is of special interest to me. I did not say English translation because it is well known that poetry cannot be translated. Rather, what we have in English is an English poem that sprang from the Chinese original and now should be considered English poetry.

How enjoyable it was for me to read through these English poems. Allow me to share with you some of my ruminations of particular poems that I found especially fine as English poems. I have mentioned above about poetry showing the physical world to us in new ways. At times I have wondered about the phenomenon of wind, which we all experience both positively, when it is hot outside, and negatively when it is cold. The poem "Wind" (p. 3), allows us to understand wind in a new light. The repetition of the question "Where is the wind?" is a good poetical device in English. Moreover, is there not a certain amount of repetition in wind itself? Further, this poem places wind in the world of nature: autumn leaves, spring flowers, waves, and bamboo. And, the participle ending of every other line suggests the blowing of the wind.

The poem "Snow" (p. 73), also deals with the physical world, presenting an aspect of which those living in colder climates have experienced. First, the poem personifies snow as a "bird" and as a "traveler," which is most apt. There is also the repetition of the word "snow" so that we can almost see the snow falling, flake by flake. The poem's conclusion is a surprise and puts the snow in the context of an old man fishing whose only catch is snow. This conclusion grants us the opportunity to consider what we have tried to "catch" and the results of which have often been contradictory to expectations.

"The Broken Hill Temple" (p. 31), takes us into the world of human creation of architecture, but places it in the context of nature. The persona of the poem moves from the outside of the temple to the inside where there is the meditation hall. The hall is "hidden behind flowering boughs." I take these "flowering boughs" to be an image of meditation, which often is the blossoming of the mind in calm contemplation. Not only does "man's cares" disappear in the meditation hall but the setting itself delights the birds of nature, an indication of the very natural dimension to the process of meditation, which is nonetheless not absolute, since its silence can be disturbed by the sound of "chimes and bells."

Poetry can also offer the viewpoint of the persona consumed with a specific concern. In "A Small Talk" (p. 49), the persona refuses to answer the question of why he lives where he does "in the green mountain" but simply describes what is around him, thus forcing the reader to answer the question for him. How many times do we ask questions without realizing that the answer is already around us? We all have singular experiences. The persona in "Abandon" (p. 39), presents his experience of loneliness after a night of drinking amidst "a shower of falling petals". What can be more lonely than a petal fallen from its flower? This is the condition of the persona of the poem when "the birds are gone and people are few." (p. 39).

Some occurrences are unique to a precise time of life. The fact of ageing is brought home to the persona in "Lines on Returning Home" (p. 9), The persona experiences, to use a word associated with the novelist James Joyce, an "epiphany" of his being now no longer the youth he was when he left home. Many of the poems in this collection express the experience of a particular moment in time as this poem does.

The experience of separated lovers is central to the poem "Musing in the Moon" (p. 6). With this poem there is both a persona and a "you." The moon common to all is all that these separated lovers can now physically share, but it becomes the basis for them perhaps to "meet... in a dream." We go from the physical world where their love began to an ethereal world where their love can be fulfilled. In "On the Passing Days" (p. 98), the moon is now the focus for the presentation of the separation of friends. The moon has not changed for the persona, nor have the "water and sky." All that has changed is that "you left." The persona knows ever so clearly that the beauty of nature without "you" present is not enough.

The above then are some of the musings I had while reading these poems. Dear reader, please take up this book and have your own experience of allowing these poems to become part of you.

Nicholas Koss; ex dean of the college of Foreign Languages and Literature, Fu Jen Catholic University Taiwan (a renowned scholar and translator, well versed in Chinese and English).

About the author

Dong Botao （董伯韜） is a freelance translator. He received a Ph.D. in classical Chinese literature from Fudan University. Dr. Dong is well versed in Chinese, English and French. His translation of the present collection of Tang poems won high critical acclaim, from renowned scholars, such as: Xie Tianzhen 谢天振 (who is the most famous scholar in translation research in PRC) and Wang Ning 王宁 (Foreign Member of Academia Europaea, Member of the Academy of Latinity).

About the book

The book is a bilingual edition of 102 Tang poems, each poem rendered into modern English and contemporary Chinese. In translating the present volume of Tang poems, whether in its modern English version or the contemporary Chinese rendering, the author did not follow the writing literally; instead, he endeavored to select only those salient grammatical structures, patterns of expression and idioms that corresponds felicitously with the original, striving in the process to convey the precise meaning, style and spirit contained in the original. As we know, Tang poetry is a timeless text that fuses aesthetics, history and philosophy – at once evocative of ancient Chinese culture and deeply relevant to contemporary concepts of beauty and nature, this volume belongs in the libraries of all serious readers.

To contact the author for information pertaining to the translation or the Tang Dynasty poems dongbotao3930@163.com

EXPLORATION ZONE

Published by Exploration Zone and Imprint of Heartspace Publications, PO Box 1085 Daylesford, Victoria 34660 Australia

Tel +61 450260348 www.heartspacebooks.com
pat@heartspacebooks.com

Copyright © 2015 Dong Botao（董伯韜）
dongbotao3930@163.com

All rights reserved under international copyright conventions. No part of this book may be reproduced, stored in a retrieval system, or transmitted in any form or by any means electronic, mechanical, photocopying, recorded or otherwise without written permission from Heartspace Publications.

Whilst every care has been taken to check the accuracy of the information in this book, the publisher cannot be held responsible for any errors, omissions or originality.

First published in 2015

ISBN 978-0-9924338-6-4

目 次 **Contents**

孔绍安 1
    落叶 Falling Leaves

韦承庆 3
    南行别弟 On the Journey South

李峤 5
    风 Wind

王 勃 7
    江亭夜月送别 Waving Goodbye? Under the Moon

陈子昂 9
    登幽州台歌 Song on Youzhou Terrace

张九龄 11
    望月怀远 Musing in the Moon
    赋得自君之出矣 Since You Went Away

王 翰 15
    凉州词 Liangzhou Song

贺知章 17
    回乡偶书 Lines On Returning Home

王 湾 19
    次北固山下 A Mooring at North Fort Hill

孟浩然 21
    春晓 Spring Morning
    宿建德江 A Mooring at Jiande River
    与诸子登岘山 On Climbing Xian Mount
    宿业师山房待丁大不至 Waiting at the Mountain Lodge

王 维 29
　　相思 Red Beans Song
　　鹿柴 The Deer Enclosure
　　竹里馆 A Cottage Amid Bamboos
　　鸟鸣涧 The Singing Birds Brook
　　白石滩 White Stone Beach
　　山中送别 Farewell
　　杂诗 Home Thought
　　阙题二首（其一）On the Mountain
　　九月九日忆山东兄弟 Sorrows on Double Ninth Day
　　渭城曲 Weicheng Song
　　辋川闲居赠裴秀才迪 A Message to Pei Di
　　山居秋暝 An Autumn Evening
　　秋夜曲 Autumn Night Song

裴 迪 55
　　留别王维 Adieu à un Ami
　　宫槐陌 A Trail

祖 咏 59
　　终南望余雪 On Seeing the Snow-peak

常 建 61
　　题破山寺后禅院 The Broken Hill Temple
　　宿王昌龄隐居 At His Retreat

寒 山 65
　　杳杳寒山道 The Cold Mountain Trail

王昌龄 67
　　出塞 At a Border Fortress
　　芙蓉楼送辛渐 Parting at Lotus Tower

王之涣 71
- 登鹳雀楼 Going up the Stork Tower
- 凉州词 Liangzhou Song

崔国辅 75
- 小长干曲 A Song of Chang Gan

李白 77
- 自遣 Abandon
- 秋风词 Lines to Autumn Wind
- 送友人 Adieu
- 渡荆门送别 At a Ferry
- 宣城见杜鹃花 Azaleas
- 夜泊牛渚怀古 A Mooring at Bull's Creek
- 早发白帝城 Farewell to the White King
- 静夜思 Homesick on a Quiet Night
- 春夜洛城闻笛 On Hearing a Flute
- 山中问答 A Small Talk
- 独坐敬亭山 Sitting Alone
- 赠汪伦 To Wang Lun
- 秋浦歌 Grey with Grief
- 黄鹤楼送孟浩然之广陵 Parting at Yellow Crane Tower
- 玉阶怨 Grief's at the Jewel Stairs

杜 甫 107
- 绝句 Quatrain
- 绝句 Quatrain
- 月夜 On a Moonlight Night
- 江南逢李龟年 A Wandering Musician

刘长卿 115
- 秋日登吴公台上寺远眺 Autumn: A View on the Terrace
- 送灵澈上人 Seeing off a Recluse
- 逢雪宿芙蓉山主人 Staying in Lotus Hill on a Snowy Night
- 听弹琴 On Hearing a Lute Player

韦应物 123
- 滁州西涧 West Brook at Chuzhou
- 秋夜寄丘员外 Lines on an Autumn Night

张 继 127
- 枫桥夜泊 An Evening Song at Maple Bridge

司空曙 129
- 江村即事 A Scene in a Riverside Village

耿 湋 131
- 秋日 One Day in the Fall

李 益 133
- 江南曲 A Complaint of Love
- 夜上受降城闻笛 On Hearing a Reed Flute

孟 郊 137
- 游子吟 Mother Love

韩 愈 139
- 早春呈水部张十八员外 Early Spring
- 晚春 Late Spring

柳宗元 143
- 江雪 Snow
- 渔翁 An Aged Fisherman

崔护 147
    题都门南庄 Last Year

王建 149
    望夫石 Petrified

刘禹锡 151
    竹枝词 The Bamboo Song
    石头城 The Stone City
    乌衣巷 Black Robe Lane

元稹 157
    行宫 At a Summer Palace

白居易 159
    赋得古原草送别 Grass on Ancient Plain
    暮江吟 The Twilight River
    问刘十九 Asking a Friend

李贺 165
    苏小小墓 She Loves Solitude

薛涛 167
    送友人 Saying Adieu, Adieu, Adieu
    风 Breeze

张祜 171
    宫词 Palace Poem

杜牧 173
    泊秦淮 A Mooring at Qinhuai River
    山行 Mountain Trip
    秋夕 An Autumn Night
    赠别 A Parting Song

李商隐 181
霜月 Frost and Moon
夜雨寄北 A Rainy Night
乐游原 Grief at Dusk
嫦娥 Lady in the Moon

温庭筠 189
瑶瑟怨 A Jade Lute

高骈 191
山亭夏日 Green

赵 嘏 193
江楼感旧 On the Passing Days

韦 庄 195
台城 The City of Tai

韩 偓 197
效崔国辅体 In Cui's Manner

鱼玄机 199
江陵愁望有寄 To—

杜荀鹤 201
送人游吴 He is Leaving

孔绍安(一首)

落叶

早秋惊落叶,飘零似客心。
翻飞未肯下,犹言惜故林。

Falling Leaves

As the leaves are
turning in the wind
in the early autumn wind
my heart is sinking
with the waves of the strangers
Nostalgia has the color
of the falling season

【诗绎】

初秋 落叶
在风中旋舞
仿佛诉说着
对树的依恋
(流浪的心
也这样飘零啊)

【品读】

天地同心,万物有情。

秋天是离别惜别的时节,也是思忆怀想的时节。诗人在对落叶的吟唱中抒写着自己对故乡对往事对亲人的追怀。

"人生无根蒂,飘如陌上尘",短短的四行诗,却熔铸了羁旅、悲秋的母题。

韦承庆(一首)

南行别弟

澹澹长江水,悠悠远客情。
落花相与恨,到地一无声。

On the Journey South

The Yangtze River flows towards the sea never to return

My parting sorrow grows endless

the blooms seem to share our grief

falling to the soil in silence

【诗绎】

奔流的长江
仿佛无尽的离愁
飘零的落花
恰似无言的别情

【品读】

远行、离别多半是感伤的。若适逢暮春,又伫立江干,那滔滔不尽的江水、飘零无已的落花,更将逗引离思万千……

诗中,落花,是即目,是环裹;长江,是远眺,是绵延。

由是,离情别绪遂相与成恨。

缺憾原是此在无时或已的操切。

李峤(一首)

风

解落三秋叶,能开二月花。
过江千尺浪,入竹万竿斜。

Wind

Where is the wind?
It's with autumn leaves falling.
Where is the wind?
It's with spring flowers blooming.
Where is the wind?
It's with waves roaring.
Where is the wind?
It's with bamboos dancing.

【诗绎】

风来自何方

风去向哪里

问飘零的秋叶

问绽放的春花

还有还有

那汹涌的巨浪

那摇曳的翠竹

【品读】

风无形。可诗人却在秋叶的静美、春花的绚烂、巨浪的雄壮、翠竹的飘逸中找寻到她的踪影……

风是神奇的,变化万千。兼具优美与崇高的风,惹人怜爱,又让人畏惧。田野里、森林中、小溪边,我们观赏着它的舞蹈,倾听着它的歌唱……

这首小诗呈现了一个观照的瞬间,从这一瞬里,传达出诗人对生命细节的凝注。

汹涌的浪,摇曳的竹给了风一种形状。风过后,留下的是空幻、空寂……

这样的体物方式与南朝宫体若合符节。未必是着意的借鉴,更可能是心灵的契合。

王勃(一首)

江亭夜月送别

乱烟笼碧砌，飞月向南端。
寂寞离亭掩，江山此夜寒。

Waving Goodbye Under the Moon

Wild mists veil the emerald steps
The moon moves towards
the southern horizon
It's quiet in the pavilion
Mountains and rivers look cold tonight

【诗绎】

夜雾
漫上台阶
月华
移向南天
离亭轻掩
今夜
江水远山
寒冷 寂寞

【品读】

送走友人后,在江畔徘徊的诗人环顾离亭,仰望明月,远眺江山,心中的孤寂怅惘油然而生。此刻,环裹着他的仅仅是深夜的清冷吗?

陆时雍《诗镜总论》说:"调入初唐,时带六朝锦色。"王勃的这首诗恰是一个例证,它的主题虽如闻一多先生所言已"从台阁走向江山朔漠",但整体风格却仍沿袭着六朝的清丽芊绵、优雅感伤。

离散的记忆,是心底的瘢痕,或隐约或明显,却永远都在。

陈子昂(一首)

登幽州台歌

前不见古人,后不见来者。
念天地之悠悠,独怆然而涕下。

Song on Youzhou Terrace

Who knows
where the ancients have been
or where the future generations will be
brooding on the endlessness
of Heaven and Earth
I stand alone in tears

【诗绎】

哪里是
往昔的圣哲
哪里是
明天的俊彦
天地悠悠
——我独立空台
为时间之伤
怆然 泪下

【品读】

高台、长天，诗人孤独地面对着无际无涯的时空，他尖锐地感知到受制于特定时、地的生命是那么无奈、那么苍凉，无论往昔的辉煌还是未来的高华，竟都与当下此刻的他无缘。

古君子"登高必赋"，诗人却只是静静地写实，而诗中那真率、朴质的美与忧伤，已静得让你心疼。

李泽厚先生认为：这是先觉者的悲哀。或然。

张九龄(二首)

望月怀远

海上生明月,天涯共此时。
情人怨遥夜,竟夕起相思。
灭烛怜光满,披衣觉露滋。
不堪盈手赠,还寝梦佳期。

Musing in the Moon

The bright moon rises on the sea
Though far away
from each other we share it
Do you know I find myself sad sleepless
and full of you in the moonlit night?
I blow out the candle and step into the court
My clothes are wet by dew
If only I handed the moonlight to you
as a gift
I return to the room hoping
to meet you in dreams

【诗绎】

碧蓝的海上生起皎洁的月轮

远隔天涯的我们共赏一泓清冷

长夜漫漫 缠绵一腔幽怨

今夕何夕 心中盈满相思

熄灭烛火走进庭前的银辉

听任露水打湿衣裳

欲掬一握如水的月华赠予

却只无奈地回到枕边

期待着梦 期待着梦中的相见

【品读】

设若阳光属于思索,那么,月华则属于思念。而思念总与另一个人的缺席联系在一起。

像《古诗十九首·明月何皎皎》的作者一样,诗人"清夜不寐""披衣""徘徊"。在互文的脉络里,诗中的思念也愈发绵长。

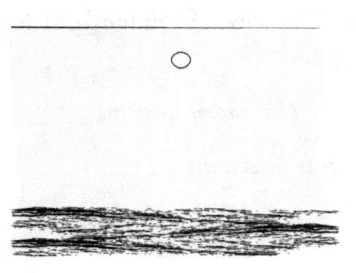

赋得自君之出矣

自君之出矣,不复理残机。
思君如满月,夜夜减清辉。

Since You Went Away

Since you went away
I have not woven the remaining cloth
My-missing-you is like the full moon
which wanes and loses
its brightness night by night

【诗绎】

你走后
我 就疏远了
机杼
只和月亮一起
夜夜 夜夜
瘦下去
只为想你

【品读】

诗中的女子诉说着自己的慵懒与憔悴。织机上尚未织就的布匹定格了那抹离别时的缺憾，而天际日渐消瘦的月华，则记录着当下的忧伤。

永井荷风在《江户艺术论》中将浮世绘的意境概括为："雨夜啼月的杜鹃，阵雨中散落的秋天树叶，落花飘风的钟声，途中日暮的山路的雪。"

诗中的意境不也一样"无常、无告、无望，使人无端嗟叹此世只是一梦"？

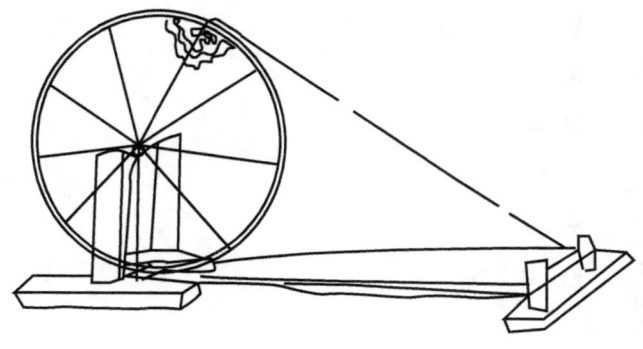

王翰（一首）

凉州词

葡萄美酒夜光杯，欲饮琵琶马上催。
醉卧沙场君莫笑，古来征战几人回。

Liangzhou Song

Sweet grape wine in shiny jade cups
Let's share a good drink
While hearing music
by Pipa girls on horseback
Do not laugh if you find us
lying drunk on the battlefield
You know how many soldiers
never return home?

【诗绎】

葡萄 是一匹魅人的兽

化身为酒

潜伏在夜光杯里

当琵琶将它唤醒

当我举杯就唇

它就奔突在我磊磊的心里

成为醉

成为遥远的乡愁

成为一声喟叹

【品读】

在苦寒的边塞,在原本寂寥的军营,一场难得的欢宴,让将士们回味起生活中的诸多美好:琵琶、美酒、夜光杯……

美及对美的渴望,就在这样精致的细节中摇曳闪烁。

而终篇豁达中的那丝感喟,则让整首诗多了一分回甘与余韵。

也许这就是明代大诗人王世贞称赞此诗为"无暇之璧"的原因?

贺知章(一首)

回乡偶书

少小离家老大回,乡音无改鬓毛衰。
儿童相见不相识,笑问客从何处来。

Lines on Returning Home

I left home young
And came back an old man
with grey temples
To my surprise
though my accents
have been unchanged
the children here saw me
and regarded me
as a traveler from afar
They asked me smiling
"Where are you from, sir?"

【诗绎】

年少时

我离开家乡

暮年后

才回到故里

此刻 鬓发斑白的我

成为孩子眼中

说着一样乡音的陌生人

他们笑着问我:"您从哪里来?"

【品读】

少小离家时该是志气满满吧?而今归来,乡音依旧,却多了几缕斑白的鬓发。流逝的光阴,给了我们一份淡泊;而那稚嫩的笑语,是否唤起曾有的纯真?

虽相隔千载,这首诗,却让我的心注满温暖与感动。它让我忘记了周遭钢筋水泥的森林,忘记了这异己的陌生的城市,而让我想起乡村路上蜿蜒的车辙,想起那次雾中的挥别,想起白桦林的枝丫上栖息的白雪和那束飘扬的黄丝带,想起……

唐诗,我精神的原乡。

王湾(一首)

次北固山下

客路青山外,行舟绿水前。
潮平两岸阔,风正一帆悬。
海日生残夜,江春入旧年。
乡书何处达,归雁洛阳边。

A Mooring at North Fort Hill

The blue mountains
snake their way
The river is smooth
a true jade-green
Its banks seem to widen
with a tide at low
And no wind stirs my lone sail
The late night gives birth to the sun
A feeling of spring seeps
from the old year
At last I can send my messengers —
Wild geese
home to Loyang

【诗绎】

青青北固山

悠悠长江水

当岸退向远方

当帆划破风

当红日升起

当夜凋零

当春意流溢

当岁华老去

那写满乡愁的信笺

是否寄达洛阳

【品读】

伴着第一缕晨曦、第一丝春意,诗人放舟于绿水之上,航向青山外的客路……

此刻,一群北归的大雁掠过夜空。诗人不由想起"雁足传书"的故事,那就托雁儿捎个信吧:雁儿啊,烦劳你飞过洛阳的时候,替我问候一下家人。

身体的流浪和心灵的归返——个中的悖反与撕扯——构成亘古的诗意。

这是一种无名的痛,一层一层在我们心头结痂。

孟浩然(四首)

春晓

春眠不觉晓,处处闻啼鸟。
夜来风雨声,花落知多少。

Spring Morning

This spring morning in bed
I find myself waking
Here and there
birds sing, sing
Last night there was wind and rain
How many flowers fell

【诗绎】

春晨
盈满鸟鸣的世界中
醒来
忆起昨夜斜风细雨
不知花落几多

【品读】

诗,是一次颖异的发现,一次华美的醒觉。

当在平凡中觅得新奇,当熟稔的生活让我们有了初遇的悸动,那一刻,我们写诗。

而读诗,又何尝不是如此?

哪怕在自幼熟读的诗中,我们也会有新的体察、新的感悟,只要我们的心还有容受美的空间与能力。

譬如,这首诗中那句"处处闻啼鸟",就是一直被我们忽略了的精彩:鸟鸣如诉,唤醒了梦中的诗人,而那美丽的一问亦于焉而生——不知风雨中,花落知多少,这织进了多少绵密婉转清新淡雅的思致。

宿建德江

移舟泊烟渚,日暮客愁新。
野旷天低树,江清月近人。

A Mooring at Jiande River

My boat is moving to moor
by a bank in the grey mist
When I find sorrow in myself
As far as I can see
a few trees appear to touch the sky
The moon in the clear water
seems nearer to me than ever

【诗绎】

黄昏 暮霭苍茫
客舟泊在无名的沙汀旁
不觉心又一次被忧愁浸湿
举目四野 远天低树
俯视清江 月影近人

【品读】

人说,寂寞是首诗。

或许寂寞中,人,更为敏感,更能静听自己心的律动。因而,在疏林里读出乡思,月影中找到欣悦。

"野旷天低树,江清月近人。"——与其说诗人在写景,毋宁说他在描摹自己的感觉。

旷野、远天,承载、覆盖着他的愁绪;清江、月色则是造物对他的抚慰。

与诸子登岘山

人事有代谢,往来成古今。
江山留胜迹,我辈复登临。
水落鱼梁浅,天寒梦泽深。
羊公碑字在,读罢泪沾襟。

On Climbing Xian Mount

Human lives succeed each other
and decay
They come and go
becoming past and present
Rivers and mountains
keep their scenic beauty
We too, climb up to have a look
The water level sinks
The fishing sluice is shallow
The weather is cold
Lake Meng-tse is deep
Lord Yang's pillar is still here
After we read it
tears soak our robes

【诗绎】

时光的花

开了又谢

今天的我们

登临昨日的江山

水落渔梁微露

天寒云梦深湛

堕泪碑泪痕依旧

——湿了我的衣襟

【品读】

诗中,交织着诗人对自然与历史的沉思与反省。

是的,山岳以其自身的恒久映衬出人类的脆弱,而碑文所铭刻的那段史迹,亦因诗人的注目而多了一层斑驳。

阅读,照亮了文本;同时,不也开启了我们自己?

虽然理解有时甚或常常是误读的别名。

宿业师山房待丁大不至

夕阳度西岭,群壑倏已暝
松月生夜凉,风泉满清听。
樵人归欲尽,烟鸟栖初定。
之子期宿来,孤琴候萝径。

Waiting at the Mountain-Lodge

The sun has set
beyond the western range
Valley after valley is shadowy and dim...
Through pine-trees comes the moon
and the coolness of evening
My ears are pure
with the songs of wind and water
Nearly all the woodcutters have got home
Birds have settled on
their perches in the mist...
Because you promised to come
I wait for you
playing lute under a wayside vine

【诗绎】

夕阳滑下山岭

暮色铺满山谷

如水的夜凉轻注松间

明月初生

风与泉在耳畔鸣响

砍柴的人走远了

暮色中鸟已归巢

朋友,你几时来呢

孤独的琴声盈满

绿萝缠绕的小径

【品读】

夕阳西下,万壑蒙烟,凉生松月,清聆风泉,樵人归尽,暮鸟栖定。与人相约,久等不至,作者独自抱琴伫立山径,静候姗姗来迟的友人,那般淡定、闲雅。

诗人最重要的天赋是爱。爱自然、爱家国。

在凡庸的散文化的世界里,得存一份深爱,葆有一腔柔情,纵然不写诗,我们不也一样诗意地栖居在大地上?

王维(十三首)

相思

红豆生南国,春来发几枝。
愿君多采撷,此物最相思。

Red Beans Song

The red beans grow in the South
Each spring they put out some new twigs
I hope you would pick many
because they stand for our friendship

【诗绎】

三月
在南国枝头
燃起的
那朵红
不正是 我们的
思念
你可会去将它
采撷 如收获
一种期盼

【品读】

思念,是一道美丽的阳光的城垣,为我们隔离开冷漠、疏远与猜忌,卫护着我们。

思念,是心中那声悠远的芦笛,当我们在生命的荒漠里踽踽独行,它为我们吟唱着远方的绿洲。

思念,是联接彼此的桥,它使我们摆脱了时空的拘执,让我们的生命超越一己品味、视界的局限,在某个刹那、某个场域神秘地交汇,彼此照亮。

两个自由的灵魂的相互思念,其实,是对他们共有的精神家园的向往或追忆。

这样的思念,超越了所有观念、法则、定理、规律,也超越了必然、因果与此在——被时间剥蚀、被空间宰制的世界。

而当这样的思念成为追忆,追忆亦随一个世代的华年萎谢之后,世界就由诗零落为散文。

那样,我们也老了。

鹿柴

空山不见人，但闻人语响。

返景入深林，复照青苔上。

The Deer Enclosure

On the lonely hills I meet no one
I hear only the echo of human voices
The sun comes in through the woods
and reaches the green moss with its light

【诗绎】

山 空空
回声 洞洞
夕阳的光线滤过树隙
静静照着青色的地衣

【品读】

鸟鸣山更幽。

偶尔的音声,愈发衬出周遭的静谧;而青苔上摇曳的日影,更给这份静谧涂上了一层怯怯的清淡。

思与境谐,情与景同。这是一首由光与影与声响成就的诗。空山、深林、青苔,这幽邃的景致是诗人恬淡、高洁的胸次的外化。

这亦是一首由禅思交织而成的诗。自南朝起,"大乘十喻"就成为诗人们喜爱的意象和题材。如"响喻,谓深山幽谷,及空舍中,若语声,若击物声,随声相应,而有响生。愚人不了,以为实有。一切音声语言,亦复如是。若有智之人,了知语音无实,心不生著,故说如响";如"影喻,谓影,但可见而不可捉。一切诸法,亦复如是。如眼耳等诸根,虽有见闻觉知,求其实体,即不可得。故说如影"。其他如"焰喻""化喻""水中月喻""镜中像喻",这些虚幻、飘渺的意象构筑了佛家对生命、对尘世充满悖论的双刃诠释:色即是空、空即是色。

当诗人郭沫若说"王维的诗有立体的透明"时,原因或就在于此吧?

竹里馆

独坐幽篁里,弹琴复长啸。
深林人不知,明月来相照。

A Cottage Amid Bamboos

Sitting alone
In the depth of the bamboos
I play the zither
and let off long whistles
Nobody appears to join me
only the bright moon drops in

【诗绎】

一个人
在这清幽的竹林
弹琴
长啸
没有别人
只有 明月
时来过访

【品读】

在静寂幽深的竹林间,诗人独坐抚琴,一曲终了,意犹未尽,乃掷琴长啸。此际,碧天的明月,仿佛在默默地静听。

皎洁的月光照亮了诗人身畔与心内的孤独。

"月亮是我故人,这世界是他乡",上世纪初,一位美国女诗人曾这样深深叹息,如果她知道十几个世纪前某个有月亮的晚上,一位东方诗人也有过相似的感喟,也许会有一份体己的温暖。

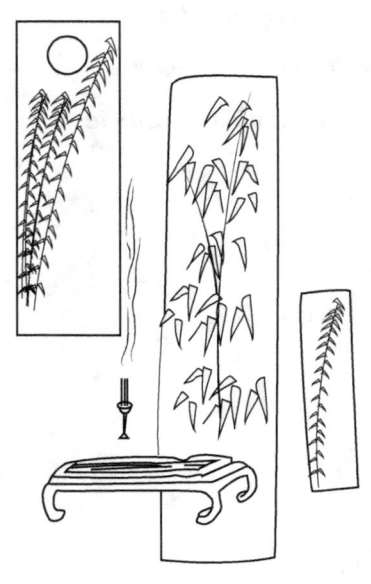

鸟鸣涧

人闲桂花落,夜静春山空。
月出惊山鸟,时鸣春涧中。

The Singing Birds' Brook

People enjoy their leisure
while the cassias are falling
Nights are calm
the spring mountains are empty
The moon moves over
and alarms the birds
Sometimes they sing
to the tune of the spring brook

【诗绎】

桂花飘逸

此身如斯安闲

夜的静谧

轻笼山的空旷

蓦地

春鸟飞鸣

和着涧水潺潺

映着月影娟娟

【品读】

花落，月出，春鸟飞鸣，涧水潺潺，这是一阕多么灵动的交响音画。而动的景物所以取得静的效果，盖缘自诗人心底的安恬与清朗。

"人闲桂花落"，在有的版本中写作"人间桂花落"，意为：月华(桂华)如水，注满人间。两相对比，各有千秋。

白石滩

清浅白石滩,绿蒲向堪把。
家住水东西,浣纱明月下。

White Stone Beach

The water at White Stone Beach is
as clear as crystal
And the green cattails are ready to be
gathered
Look, girls are rinsing yarn in the moonlight
It is said that their homes are
in the neighborhood

【诗绎】

白石滩的水清清浅浅
水下的蒲草绿意盈盈
那月下浣纱的女子
她的居所就在左近

【品读】

白石滩恍若一个水晶世界,那月下浣纱的女子,仿佛一并拥有了水之清、蒲之韧、月之明、石之洁,而水与蒲、与月、与石也似乎拥有了女子的温婉、明秀。

本诗选自王维的名作《辋川集》。清代诗人王渔洋说:"王、裴辋川绝句,句句入禅。""妙谛微言,与世尊拈花,迦叶微笑,等无差别。"

我想,这里的禅,既是诗人心手相应、与物从容的书写样貌,也是读者直指心源、了无牵碍的阅读体验。

山中送别

山中相送罢,日暮掩柴扉。
春草明年绿,王孙归不归?

Farewell

*Seeing you out on the mountain
at sunset
I close the wooden fence door
When grass turns green again
in the coming spring
Will you return, my friend?*

【诗绎】

你走向山外

我把暮色掩入门扉

你会回来吗 朋友

当春天芳草绿满天涯

【品读】

像画中的留白,诗人将话别、惜别的依依情怀,都留给了我们去想象,而只是淡淡地勾描出自己别后独处时的怅惘与憧憬。那么简约,那么深挚!

"海内存知己,天涯若比邻。""请君试问东流水,别意与之谁短长。""剪不断、理还乱,是离愁,别是一番滋味在心头。""离恨恰如春草,更行更远还生。"……虽然豪迈、婉约有别,诗人们却有着一样的赤子情怀,因而也就总是能比我们更深入地体悟人生,体悟热烈背后的无常。

试问哪一次相逢不是以离别作结?!

杂诗

君自故乡来，应知故乡事。
来日绮窗前，寒梅著花未？

Home Thought

You come from our hometown
You ought to know what's going on there
When you left
the winter plum was blooming
outside my silk-paned window

【诗绎】

来自故乡的你

想必知道那里的境况

你来的时候

窗前的那树寒梅在开吗?

【品读】

一些极细小、极微末的情事,往往引发我们对家的怀想。

鲁迅先生在《朝花夕拾》小引中写道:"我有一时,曾经屡次忆起儿时在故乡所吃的蔬果:菱角、罗汉豆、茭白、香瓜。凡这些,都是极其鲜美可口的;都曾是使我思乡的蛊惑。后来,我在久别之后尝到了,也不过如此;唯独在记忆上,还有旧来的意味存留。他们也许要哄骗我一生,使我时时反顾。"

诗中绮窗前的那树寒梅怕也要在诗人的记忆上存留一生了,作为乡愁的诱因与象征。

阙题二首(其一)

荆豀白石出,天寒红叶稀。
山路元无雨,空翠湿人衣。

On the Mountain

Jing creek is so shallow and clear
That one can see white pebbles in the water
As it gets colder and colder
only a few red leaves remains on the boughs
It isn't rain but blue emptiness
that will wet one's cloak

【诗绎】

天冷了
走在荆溪边
走在山路上
水底卵石莹白
枝头红叶稀疏
苍翠的流岚
打湿我们衣裳
如雨

【品读】

台湾著名诗人、画家席慕容女士曾经说过：若是一个孩子，没有用手触摸过树干，用脚踩过落叶，她就无法教他绘画，因为他没有直接面对美的经验。

是的。只有体验过苍翠欲滴、湿衣如雨的暮霭朝岚，我们才知道什么是"山色"！

九月九日忆山东兄弟

独在异乡为异客,每逢佳节倍思亲。
遥知兄弟登高处,遍插茱萸少一人。

Sorrows on Double Ninth Day

Alone in a strange place
I am the stranger here
On festivals I miss doubly
Those near and dear
I know you're climbing
the mount wearing dogwood
How I wish I were among you there

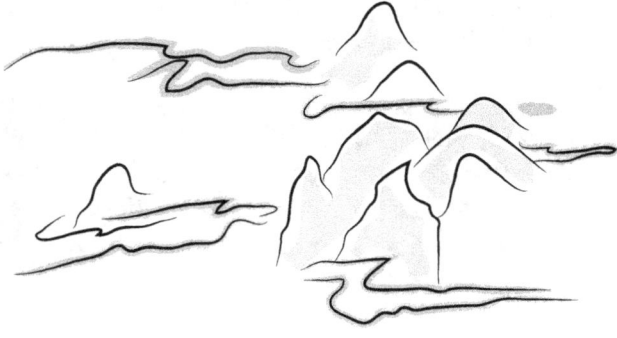

【诗绎】

当我独自在异乡

在陌生人中流浪

每逢佳节

我总是越发想念亲人

今天我故乡的兄弟

正插戴着茱萸 在山间畅游

我却独自在异乡

在陌生人中流浪

【品读】

王维的《九月九日忆山东兄弟》，总是令我想起英国浪漫主义诗人华滋华斯的名句："当我来到海外/在陌生人中旅行/英格兰，我才知道/我赋予你的是何等的爱。"

也许离别恰是反向的归返，时空的距离，让我们有了审视与回味的空间，我们因而发现了平日里忽略了的温馨与爱。

相传这首《九月九日忆山东兄弟》是诗人十七岁时写的。当时，他刚刚离开家乡，年轻的心初解乡愁。"每逢佳节倍思亲"，这淡雅、隽永的诗句，千百年来，不知触动了多少游子的心。

渭城曲

渭城朝雨浥轻尘,客舍青青柳色新。
劝君更尽一杯酒,西出阳关无故人。

Weicheng Song

It's morning
and Weicheng is bathing in the rain
The guesthouse and the willows
look fresh and green
Let's have one more for the road
Out west, beyond Fort Yangguan
there are no friends like us

【诗绎】

客舍的屋瓦青青
路边的垂柳盈盈
春晨 雨染绿了渭城
知心的老友
请再干一杯香醇的美酒
阳关外 这样平凡的快乐也难求

【品读】

一个春天的清晨,王维送别好友元二出使安西。淅沥的雨声,似乎在诉说、在叹息;依依的垂柳仿佛在挽留、在叮咛:朋友,保重!

《渭城曲》又名《送元二使安西》《阳关三叠》,是唐代送别诗中的名篇。哀而不伤、动中法度,全诗浸润着"静穆的伟大、崇高的单纯",凝结着素朴、简约、优雅的古典美。

"悲莫悲兮生别离。""春草碧色,春水绿波;送君南浦,伤如之何?"与江淹《别赋》的一味感伤不同,《渭城曲》的可贵之处在于诗中的离情给予我们的不只是惆怅,还有更深的生之感召。

辋川闲居赠裴秀才迪

寒山转苍翠,秋水日潺湲。

倚杖柴门外,临风听暮蝉。

渡头馀落日,墟里上孤烟。

复值接舆醉,狂歌五柳前。

A Message to Pei Di

The mountains are cold and blue now

and the autumn waters have run all day

By my thatch door, leaning on my staff

I listen to cicadas in the evening wind

Sunset lingers at the ferry

Supper-smoke float from the houses

Oh, dear friend

how glad I am to hear you

sing a wild song over wine

【诗绎】

一带寒山郁郁苍苍

秋水潺潺流走时光

我倚杖伫立在柴门外

晚风轻送暮蝉的吟唱

那朵夕阳在渡头绽放

炊烟缕缕 袅袅升起

接舆 陶潜 我和你

一同欢歌 畅饮

【品读】

寒山、秋水、落日、孤烟构成一幅和谐静谧的田园风光。而柴门倚杖,临风听蝉,诗人的意态又是多么安闲、洒脱。

在这个秋日的黄昏,诗人和友人一起享受着放浪形骸、脱略桎梏的快乐。一时间,诗人似乎产生了某种幻觉,仿佛接舆、陶潜,这两位著名的隐者,也来到了他们身畔,与他们一同畅饮、放歌。

这是久被禁锢的心灵觉醒后的吟唱!

山居秋暝

空山新雨后，天气晚来秋。
明月松间照，清泉石上流。
竹喧归浣女，莲动下渔舟。
随意春芳歇，王孙自可留。

An Autumn Evening

After evening rain
the mountain fades into a void
filled with autumnal coolness
Moonlight lingers in the pines
Crystal brooks flow over stone
Bamboos whisper of washing-girls
who are bound for home
Lotus-leaves yield before a fisher-boat
And what does it matter
that springtime has gone
while you are here
O Prince of Friends

【诗绎】

黄昏 刚刚落了一场雨

空灵的山间更多秋意

明媚的月光在松林里照耀

清澈的泉水在岩石上流淌

竹林里传来洗衣女子的笑语

荷叶摇曳间渔舟划过

就任凭花叶飘零吧

只要我们能彼此相伴

【品读】

明月清泉,竹喧莲动,浣女归舟——雨后的秋山多么清丽,多么富于生机。

苏轼说:"味摩诘之诗,诗中有画。"如果把这首诗视作一幅画,它的色彩集中于柔和的绿色(松)、蓝色(泉)、黄色(月)、红色(莲)。红色、黄色映衬着淡淡的蓝色,使得画面有了深度与对比,而碧水长天更赋予整幅画一种平衡与绵延不尽之感。

秋夜曲

桂魄初生秋露微，轻罗已薄未更衣。
银筝夜久殷勤弄，心怯空房不忍归。

Autumn Night Song

Under the new-born moon
she plays the silver lute
in the courtyard endlessly
Her silk dress, too flimsy
For the autumn dew
However, she isn't willing to ao back
to the empty room
that is an emotional void

【诗绎】

一钩新月
镂刻着秋意
白露茫茫
点染了罗衫
夜色流过琴弦
空旷的房间
注满寂寞
……

【品读】

新月、白露、银筝、罗衫……诗人用它们编织成一份难言的寂寞。

于是,这寂寞有了新月的形状、白露的光泽、银筝的音声、罗衫的质感,变得立体而又有诗意。

王维的诗,要慢慢读,慢慢想,诗里没有大喜大悲,甚至看不出情绪的起落,但也并不就是"淡"——难抑的寂寞与哀伤,像筝声,在指间流走了。

裴迪（二首）

留别王维

归山深浅去，　须尽丘壑美。
莫学武陵人，　暂游桃源里。

Adieu à un Ami

Since you chose to return there
feast your eyes on this maze of mounts
Do you remember the fisherman?
He is not a native
from the Peach-Blossom wonderland
but a traveler from the wasteland

【诗绎】

既然回归山林
那就尽享丘壑之美吧
可不要学那位武陵渔人
只是匆匆地游过桃花源

【品读】

美国诗人弗罗斯特在《林中路》一诗中写道:

黄色的树林里分出两条路/可我却不能同时徜徉/多年以后在某个地方/……我将轻声叹息将往事讲述/一片树林里分出两条路/而我选择了更少人走的一条/而这成就了所有的不同(Two roads diverged in yellow wood/And sorry I could not travel both/……I shall be telling this with a sigh/Somewhere ages and ages hence/Two roads diverged in a wood, and I/I took the one less traveled by/And that has made all the difference)

与对财富、权力的追寻相比,回归山林、息影林泉,无疑是一条更少人走的路,选择它自然需要更多的淡定与从容。

而诗人总是自觉地踏上荒寒的旅程, 怀着乡愁,寻找心灵的原乡。

宫槐陌

门前宫槐陌，是向欹湖道。
秋来山雨多，落叶无人扫。

A Trail

Outside the gate there is
A trail to the lake
through the ash trees
Since the autumn came
it has rained much amid the mount
The fallen leaves envelope the trail
No one sweeps them

【诗绎】

门
开向欹湖
路
植满宫槐
落叶
覆满小径
只缘秋来
山雨渐多

【品读】

清幽、静寂。这份清幽、静寂属于小径、宫槐、秋雨、落叶，属于隐居其间的诗人，属于他那颗能够感悟雨滴之静的诗心。

诗人鲍尔吉·原野说　自己是个小偷，只从造化偷得一点东西，但因为这东西太美好，要展示出来，让大家看到才能满足成就感。

对此，裴迪想必深有会心，所以，他才让静谧唱出这样曼妙的歌。

祖咏(一首)

终南望余雪

终南阴岭秀,积雪浮云端。
林表明霁色,城中增暮寒。

On Seeing the Snow-peak

See how Zhongnan Mountain soars
with its white top towering the skies
The sunshine after
the snow is glowing the tree
The dusk finds cold creeping
in the city slow

【诗绎】

山

冲向

白雪与云

结成的天际线

雪晴的明丽

绽放在林端

清寒了暮色几分

【品读】

盛唐,以诗赋取士。

据《唐诗纪事》载,《终南望余雪》是祖咏考进士时的应试诗。按照规则,应试诗应该写五言六韵十二句,但祖咏写完这四句后却没有继续写下去。考官问他为什么,他回答说:"意尽。"

多么至情至性的诗人啊!

他超越了现世的成败,而遥遥注目覆满白雪的山巅……

在那里,时间凝结了,韶华与美好不再流逝。

常建(二首)

题破山寺后禅院

清晨入古寺，初日照高林。
竹径通幽处，禅房花木深。
山光悦鸟性，潭影空人心。
万籁此都寂，但余钟磬音。

The Broken Hill Temple

At dawn I come to an old temple
as the first rays of the sun glows the treetops
A path along the bamboo grove
Leads to a quiet place—
a meditation hall
hidden behind flowering boughs
Here, mountain scenery delights the birds
and the reflections in the pond
Empty a man's cares
All the sounds melt into silence
but for the echoes of chimes and bells

【诗绎】

清晨 结成
透明的网
在古寺 林间
筛落一朵朵
初生的阳光

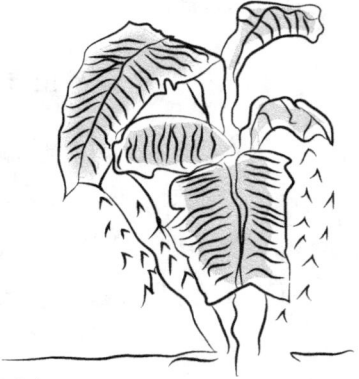

竹径清幽
通向 花木掩映的禅室
一泓清潭 一泓山光 一泓鸟啼
清清 轻轻 注入
钟磬悠杳的和音 远漾

【品读】

宁静,是生命的神韵。

它是那么悠远、那么深邃,不是我们的眼睛可以凝视、耳朵可以谛听、嘴唇可以品尝的。

宁静,要用心来体悟。

虚、静、空、白间律动着一缕诗情、一丝禅悟。

宿王昌龄隐居

清溪深不测，隐处唯孤云。
松际露微月，清光犹为君。
茅亭宿花影，药院滋苔纹。
余亦谢时去，西山鸾鹤群。

At His Retreat

By a clear deep lake
your retreat lies among the clouds
And through the pines
the moon appears half
whose light mirrors
your own pure-hearted friend
You rest under thatch
In the shadow of your flowers
Your dewy herbs flourish
in their bed of moss
Let me leave the world like you
on your western mountain
with phoenixes and cranes

【诗绎】

清溪之水　幽深难测

隐于其所　孤云卷舒

松林之间　明月半规

清辉熠熠　为君皎洁

茅亭之畔　花影扶疏

药院栏边　苔藓滋生

谢世绝俗　归隐西山

与鸾鹤为友　伴君幽独

【品读】

尘世中，人与人之间的疏离、隔绝也许是常态。

但，诗人却执着于心灵的契合。

他们不汲汲于无谓的声名、无常的毁誉，但却钟情于会心的谛视、倾心的晤谈……

月光皴染着松林，风轻轻流过，可以想见两位诗人在树叶细语间的悄然漫步，该多么惬意。

风景为他们言说着那深于一切言语的相知相惜。

寒山(一首)

杳杳寒山道

杳杳寒山道,落落冷涧滨。

啾啾常有鸟,寂寂更无人。

淅淅风吹面,纷纷雪积身。

朝朝不见日,岁岁不知春。

The Cold Mountain Trail

Winding and winding—the Cold Mountain Trail

Bleak and bleak—the icy creek bank

Chirping, Chirping—always birds

Quiet, quiet—nobody else

Whip, whip—the wind slaps my face

Whirled and tumbled—snow piles on my back

Morning after morning

one doesn't see the sun

Year after year

there is no sign of spring

【诗绎】

深幽的山径

孤寂的涧边

看不见人影

只听到鸟鸣

风吹打着我的面庞

雪落满全身

清晨见不到太阳

一年又一年

没有春的痕迹

【品读】

寒山诗中的自然环境清冷、孤寂，但他的心境却是安宁、淡泊的。那是面对生命大全时的静默，在静默中注心倾聆真与善与美的香颂。

此刻，灯前，回望岁月的那端，我仿佛看到那流浪的僧人正在风雪中踽踽独行。在那无所凭依的孤独里，没有示弱，没有自怜，只有在苦难中虔心低首的宁谧。

那宁谧，我们暌违了多久了？

王昌龄（二首）

出塞

秦时明月汉时关，万里长征人未还。
但使龙城飞将在，不教胡马度阴山。

At a Border Fortress

The moon shines the pass as always
None of the soldiers
from the long march ever return
If the winged general stationed
in the Dragon city
The Tartar horsemen would never
have dared to cross the Yin Mountain

【诗绎】

明月 关隘不改秦汉的雄壮
跋涉万里的征人戍守着边疆
我们的将领若是飞将军李广
鞑靼的马蹄怎还能越过阴山

【品读】

定型于梁朝的边塞诗,最初,源于南朝诗人对遥远北方的浪漫想象。

那原是故国的北方,不知何时,却成为了异地。

历史似乎总是这样:北方征服了南方,南方却书写着北方。

逮至盛唐,诗人们的笔下依然斑斓着史籍中边远的地名,虽然此时这些名词新的所指是——中亚。

与前代不同,无论王昌龄、王之涣,还是王翰、李颀,盛唐诗人们的边塞诗总是洋溢着一种昂扬奋发的生命格调。

那是盛唐气象,少年精神的写真。

芙蓉楼送辛渐

寒雨连江夜入吴,平明送客楚山孤。
洛阳亲友如相问,一片冰心在玉壶。

Parting at Lotus Tower

In the chilly night rain
I sailed the Wu with you
The dawn found me seeing you off
against the Chu Mountains
looking like saying goodbye
to you in sorrow
"Friend, if my folks and others
ask about me in Luoyang
tell them my heart is as pure as ice
in a jade vase.

【诗绎】

凄寒的夜雨

滴破

如梦的吴江

黎明时分

你离去 远望楚山

是那般孤冷 朋友啊

洛阳亲友 若是问起

就请告诉他们 我心皎洁

直若玉壶冰

【品读】

"寒雨连江夜入吴"一句中的"入"写微雨悄然来临,与杜甫《春夜喜雨》中"随风潜入夜"中的"入"字用法相同。

夜雨蒙蒙,弥漫了整个江面,诗人在芙蓉楼为友人辛渐饯别。临行依依,诗人殷殷嘱托"洛阳亲友如相问,一片冰心在玉壶",碌碌尘世,浮名、虚利,都可淡然置之,而高洁的人格、纯净的心灵,却是要永远持存的。

这是一场真实的雨,淋湿了衣服,上涨了江水;这是一场灵魂的雨,汰去了阴郁,冲走了感伤。临别时,"一片冰心"的叮咛,回荡在楚山吴水间,也回荡在千载以下读者的心间。

王之涣(二首)

登鹳雀楼

白日依山尽,黄河入海流。
欲穷千里目,更上一层楼。

Going up the Stork Tower

The setting sun dips behind the mounts
The Yellow River rushes out to sea
To take a better view
of things out there
we should climb one more flight of stair

【诗绎】

夕阳
落下了山梁
黄河
奔流进大海
若要俯瞰千里奇观
就让我们再上层楼

【品读】

"白日依山尽,黄河入海流",诗的前两句写楼周围的景物,第四句写登楼之人,而将物与人连接在一起的是第三句。

"欲穷千里目",诗人的目光追随着夕阳、夕阳辉映下的滚滚黄河,进而,产生了更上层楼的愿望、俯瞰千里的愿望。

这正是本诗的可贵之处——它将宏阔而富于哲思的胸襟与诗歌的表现艺术完美地结合在了一起。

凉州词

黄河远上白云间,一片孤城万仞山。
羌笛何须怨杨柳,春风不度玉门关。

Liangzhou Song

The Yellow River
stretches to the sky
A lone fort sits
among many mountains
The Qiang flute
need not envy the willow tree
The spring breeze never sweeps
beyond Gate Yumen

【诗绎】

荒寒的玉门

巍峨的群山

远望去

黄河奔流向云间

吹笛人啊,你何必吹响那阕《怨杨柳》

难道 难道你忘了这是塞上

没有春天

【品读】

长河、白云、群山、孤城。

一片萧索、枯寒中,诗人又有着怎样的感怀?也许就像那曲《怨杨柳》吧:纵然忧伤,也有希望的执着。

从流传下来的作品看,王之涣在他的同代人中,也许最沉湎于边塞梦幻。

他对于边塞风光充满向往,那茫茫瀚海流溢着苦涩的美感、壮美的诗情……这也许就是诗人林庚所说的"盛唐气象、少年精神"吧?

崔国辅(一首)

小长干曲

月暗送湖风,相寻路不通。
菱歌唱不彻,知在此塘中。

A Song of Chang Gan

The moonlight looks dim
as the tide farewells the breeze
How hard it is to find where you are
I know, I can reach you
because there are your songs to follow

【诗绎】

月色迷蒙
晚风轻送潮信
此刻 心上的人啊
你在何方
莲叶田田
悠扬的歌声
领我找寻你的方向

【品读】

在月光的牵引下,暮潮奔涌。

诗中的男子在江上找寻着自己的恋人,虽然他并不知道她的所在,但那熟悉的美妙歌声却让他坚信他们会相见。

南朝乐府中的女子,总是那样清丽,像莲、像蘋、像菱。

"最是那一低头的温柔/像一朵水莲花/不胜凉风的娇羞。"当徐志摩写下这曼丽的诗句时,我想,在他心湖荡漾的许就是这采菱女子的倩影。

李白（十五首）

自遣

对酒不觉暝，落花盈我衣。
醉起步溪月，鸟还人亦稀。

Abandon

Night had fallen before I knew it

I was drinking in a shower of falling petals

I staggered, to walk to the brook by moonlight

The birds are gone and people are few

【诗绎】

暝色里
落花如雨
独饮的我
扶醉走向溪边
那儿已看不到人影
与飞鸟的痕迹
只有月光轻漾在波心

【品读】

在诗中,李白自况为一位饮者、侠客、狂士、谪仙人。

他是那么飘逸、不羁,就像他最爱的月光,永是皎洁,永是纯净。

在暝色里,在晦暗与光明的交口,在暧昧与清晰的重叠处,诗人伫立着。

是有所期待,还是茫然怀想?

历史无语,由是,诗开始言说。

秋风词

秋风清,秋月明,

落叶聚还散,寒鸦栖复惊。

相思相见知何日,此时此夜难为情。

Lines to Autumn Wind

Clean fall wind

Clear fall moon

Leaves heaped and scattered

By the wind

A cold raven

flaps slowly

from his roost

When and where

shall I see you again

do you know?

I cannot help think of you tonight

【诗绎】

秋风秋月

那般清明

洒落一地的叶子

聚了又散

归巢的寒鸦

已复惊醒

哦，几时 几时

我们再见

你可知 可知

我今夜的忧伤

【品读】

"相思相见知何日，此时此夜难为情"，在哀愁、幽怨与无奈中，深蕴一脉依依的心怀，热烈、持久、温暖。

这样的感觉，读来竟有些像《诗经》。"蒹葭苍苍，白露为霜；所谓伊人，在水一方。"

所思是一样迢遥，一样纯净。

"大雅久不作，吾衰竟谁陈？"——对李白而言，中国君子原初的精神感觉，宛如那片永恒的月色，照亮生命的子夜。

送友人

青山横北郭,白水绕东城。
此地一为别,孤蓬万里征。
浮云游子意,落日故人情。
挥手自兹去,萧萧班马鸣。

Adieu

With a blue line of mountains north of the wall

And east of the city a white curve of water

Here you must leave me

to drift away

like a loosened water-plant

Hundreds of miles...

Dusk will find you and me

like a floating cloud

Think of each other

Waving, we say good-bye

as my horse neighs

again and again

【诗绎】

青山横卧北郭

白水环绕东城

游子是种无根的植物

背负着思念远行

浮云落日下

我们是否会想起

今天萧萧马鸣里

我们曾挥手别离

【品读】

"黯然销魂者,唯别而已矣。"

江淹哀婉的吟唱成为多少后世诗人灵感的源头。

但李白的送别诗却突破了这种"有别必怨,有怨必盈"的情感模式。

他总是以自己独特的个性气质,在这特定的时间和特定的场景下描摹不同的存在样貌与精神境界。

那是盛唐气象与少年精神的结晶。

渡荆门送别

渡远荆门外，来从楚国游。
山随平野尽，江入大荒流。
月下飞天镜，云生结海楼。
仍怜故乡水，万里送行舟。

At a Ferry

Sailing far off from Jingmen Ferry
Soon I shall be with people in the south
Where the mountains end
and the plains begin
Where river winds through wilderness...
The moon lifts, like a mirror
Sea-clouds gleam like palaces
And the water has brought me
a touch of home
How well I enjoy her company

【诗绎】

轻轻地 我

离开荆门来到楚地

山退远了平芜拓向天际

江水 流入大荒

月像明镜在流转

云在天空 书写

海市蜃楼的传说

依依的江水啊 你多么可爱

遥遥万里 伴着我流浪

【品读】

从高山到平原,长江用它最最母性的鼻音,为诗人哼唱一阕最最温馨的民谣。

伴他远行。

此刻,晕黄的灯下,我仿佛看到他在时光之河的那端回身轻轻向我问道:"你可曾听过那最最母性的鼻音?"

是的,我听过。

在他清雄飘逸的诗篇里,听过。

宣城见杜鹃花

蜀国曾闻子规鸟，宣城还见杜鹃花。
一叫一回肠一断，三春三月忆三巴。

Azaleas

In the Country of Shu
I used to hear the nightjar
In the city of Xuancheng
I see again the azaleas in bloom
One call
One turn
One broken heart...
In the third spring moon
In the third month
I remember the three lands of Pa

【诗绎】

蜀国的子规歌声婉转

宣城的杜鹃花开艳丽

记忆里的歌声让我愁肠百结

眼前的春色令我思忆万千

【品读】

杜鹃,又名子规,暮春时节,它哀婉地吟唱着"不如归去、不如归去……"

那沥血的歌声染红了漫山遍野的杜鹃花。

我们一提起杜鹃,心头眼底便好像有说不尽的诗意。

它本身不用说,已经是望帝的化身了。有时又被认为薄命的佳人,忧国的志士;声是满腹乡思,血是遍山踯躅;可怜、哀婉、纯洁、至诚……在人们的心目中成为了爱的象征。这爱的象征似乎已经成为了民族的感情。

而且,这种感情还超越了民族的范围,东方诸国大都受到了感染。例如日本,杜鹃在文学上所占的地位,并不亚于中国。

同样来自巴蜀的李白当然是知晓这些传说的,所以子规鸟与杜鹃花一起浸染了他的乡愁。

夜泊牛渚怀古

牛渚西江夜,青天无片云。
登舟望秋月,空忆谢将军。
余亦能高咏,斯人不可闻。
明朝挂帆席,枫叶落纷纷。

A Mooring at Bull's Creek

At Bull's creek
On Western River
The night sky is blue and cloudless
I go on deck to watch the bright moon
I cannot help think of the late General Xie
As you know
I also compose poetry…
… but that man's like
will not be found again
In the morning
I shall make sail
And say good-bye to the maples
Their leaves fall, shower by shower

【诗绎】

深夜

在西江

牛渚

碧蓝的夜空

没有一丝云彩

我登上小船

远眺天边的那轮明月

想起谢尚、袁宏

我也能

高声歌咏瑰丽的诗篇

却没有那样的知遇

明朝枫叶飘零之顷

我又将离开这里远行

【品读】

李白是位爱月的诗人。

一个明月如霜好风如水的秋夜,他静静地伫立在清江边,隔着遥远的岁月,与时间那头的古人对话。

这真挚而美好的怀想之情,是多么清新、隽永。

早发白帝城

朝辞白帝彩云间,千里江陵一日还。
两岸猿声啼不住,轻舟已过万重山。

Farewell to the White King

Dawn found me
saying good-bye to the White King
Under the rosy sky
to sail thousands of miles
back to Jiangling on that day
The crying of monkeys from the shores
followed all the way
Lightly, my boat was speeding
past a sea of mountains high

【诗绎】

清晨 我辞别了云蒸霞蔚的白帝城

黄昏 回到了千里之外的江陵

两岸的猿声不住啼唤

苍山如海

轻快的小舟驶过那波涛万顷

【品读】

青山碧水间,疾驶如飞的小舟、迤逦不绝的猿声……在这份飘逸飞动中,洋溢着诗人历经人生的百转千回后喷薄而出的一种豪情与欢悦!

诗是无处不在的,在黄河岸边、在扬子江头、在放逐的路上,乃至逼仄的陋室。

生命中的伤,在诗中疗治。

诗,亦是无时不在的。不仅年少时,有诗;当鬓染飞霜时,依然有诗。

诗是发现。在熟识或陌生的生命中,找到美与真与善。

诗随着诗人的成长而丰盈。在太白的诗里,我们看到,诗人越向前行,诗越纯净,越无邪!

静夜思

床前明月光,疑是地上霜。
举头望明月,低头思故乡。

Homesick on a Quiet Night

The bright moonlight near my cot
seems to me like white ground frost
I look up to gaze at the moon
I look down to think of home

【诗绎】

清冷的月光
洒满床前
就像地上结了秋霜
抬头复低头
悠悠地
我望着那明月啊
想起故乡

【品读】

夜深了,月光透过窗棂,乍一看,仿佛是在地上涂了一层皑皑的浓霜。

望着那轮皎洁清冷的秋月,客居的诗人想起远隔千里的故乡,想起故乡的亲人……他的头不觉默默地低了下去。

从来没有哪位诗人像李白这样钟情于月亮也从来没有哪位诗人让我们看到与我们这样切近的月亮。

在他的诗中月亮与我们的距离不再以光年度量如同在他的诗中他与我们从未远隔千载。

因为他总是可以击中我们痛或快乐的所在让我们莞尔让我们泪下让我们额首让我们扼腕。

我们与他素昧平生他却能抵达我们心的深处与我们在沉默中倾谈莫逆一笑。

春夜洛城闻笛

谁家玉笛暗飞声,散入春风满洛城。
今夜曲中闻折柳,何人不起故园情。

On Hearing a Flute

Where does the sound
of a distant jade flute come from
It is on the spring wind
to fill Luoyang
Who can help
but long for his homeland
should he hear
The willow—
Breaking song tonight

【诗绎】

从哪里传来

这幽怨的笛声

乘着春风洒满洛城

今夜 多少游子

在这凄婉的曲调中

想起故乡

【品读】

诗人客居洛阳。某个春天的晚上,不经意地听到城中某处传来悠扬的笛声,细听之下,竟是忧伤的《折杨柳》。在唐代,民间有折柳送别、折柳赠远的习俗。

柳,与"留"谐音,象征着一种思绪、一种期冀。于是,诗人不禁想到所有客居的旅人,若是听到这笛声,他们也会兴起浓浓的乡愁吧?

山中问答

问余何意栖碧山,笑而不答心自闲。
桃花流水窅然去,别有天地非人间。

A Small Talk

You ask me why I live
in these green mountains
I smile, and cannot answer
I am completely at ease
A peach blossom is flowing on the current
an earthly paradise under the sun

【诗绎】

你问我为什么
在这里流连
既无以言说心下的悠闲
淡然一笑可否算作回答
粉红的桃花清泠的流水
你该知道
这是另一个天地 迥异人间

【品读】

李白是一位真正的韵在骨子里的诗人。

他的诗的美并不在于技巧、词句,甚至不在于气势、想象,而在于他所独有的那种"清水出芙蓉,天然去雕饰"的仪态。

真、纯的人格特质在我们的文化里是那么稀缺,李诗亦因而可贵。

独坐敬亭山

众鸟高飞尽，孤云独去闲。
相看两不厌，只有敬亭山。

Sitting Alone

All birds have flown out of sight
A lonely cloud is drifting at ease
Now only Jingting Mount and me
never be tired of looking at each other

【诗绎】

众多的鸟儿都已飞远
不见了踪影
而孤独的云朵
还在天空闲闲地飘荡
此刻默默相对，未曾厌倦的
只有我和敬亭山

【品读】

诗中,李白诉说着一种难以言传的孤独。

如果"采菊东篱下,悠然见南山"的陶潜是李白伟大的先行者,那么,"我见青山多妩媚,料青山、见我应如是"的辛弃疾就是他杰出的后辈。

是的,他们的孤独所以只有广袤、博大的自然才能包容,才能消解,是因为他们的孤独本就不是源于一己的穷愁。

赠汪伦

李白乘舟将欲行，忽闻岸上踏歌声。
桃花潭水深千尺，不及汪伦送我情。

To Wang Lun

My boat is about to leave
when I hear your farewell songs on shore
Nobody can tell how deep
the Lake of Peach Blossom may be
But I'm sure it's not
so deep as your friendship for me

【诗绎】

刚刚要解缆前行

岸上传来你的踏歌声

清澈的桃花潭深达千尺

却比不上你的情谊

【品读】

"桃花潭水深千尺,不及汪伦送我情。"

"生不用封万户侯,但愿一识韩荆州。"

诗人是多么看重节操,看重彼此相知相惜的情怀!在明白如话的诗行里,流淌着的是深挚的情谊;它如清清潭水,涤尽一切华丽与矫揉,从而映出友情的纯真、本色。

秋浦歌

白发三千丈,缘愁似个长。
不知明镜里,何处得秋霜。

Grey with Grief

My whitening hair streams
As long as my sadness does
Looking at myself in the mirror
I'm wondering when and where
I took on this hoary frost

【诗绎】

岁月消尽
已无从忆起
是什么时候 又在哪里
鬓边第一次发现了白雪的痕迹
只默默地看镜中自己
那为苍老的忧愁
漂染的发丝
宛如秋霜绵延千里

【品读】

明镜、秋霜,纵使在书写忧愁,李白也总是选择这样晶莹剔透的意象。这是诗人纯真光明的人格的写照。因为有了这纯真与光明,他才能够不为忧愁的阴影遮蔽。

也许是这位连字都是"太白"的诗人的宿命,"白色"萦绕于他的诗句之间。在他笔下,不仅云、水、鸥、鸟被写成白色,浪、雨、猿、龟,甚至彩虹、太阳也都被描绘成白色!

最平凡与最珍贵的事物都沉浸在这片茫茫白色里。

而青莲笔下的"白",不仅是一种颜色,更是"纯洁""明净""清澈"的能指。

本诗中,"白"虽只用以描摹发色,明镜和秋霜却也因了一样的明净、清澈而予人以立体的透明。

白,隐喻着道之至味与天之无偏。

黄鹤楼送孟浩然之广陵

故人西辞黄鹤楼,烟花三月下扬州。
孤帆远影碧空尽,唯见长江天际流。

Parting at Yellow Crane Tower

My friend has left
the Yellow Crane Tower
and headed east to Yangzhou
In the month of flowers and mist
his lone sail fades
into the vast blue sky
Standing still, I watch
the Yangtse River rolling by

【诗绎】

你走了
我在楼边伫立着
看 那孤独的帆儿
从三月的岸边划过
恰似如烟的柳花
一<u>丝丝</u> 一<u>丝丝</u>
溶入蔚蓝的天际

【品读】

两位漂泊经年的诗人异地相逢又要离别。

然而，他们没有忧伤，没有怨艾，甚至不去希求上苍对彼此的赐福。

因为，难舍须舍。他们知道。

玉阶怨

玉阶生白露,夜久侵罗袜。
却下水晶帘,玲珑望秋月。

Grief at the Jewel Stairs

The jewel steps are already wet with dew
It is so late that my silk stockings
have been soaked before I know
and I let fall the crystal curtain
and watch the clear autumn moon

【诗绎】

玉阶上
凝结着
点点白露
夜深时分
露水浸湿了罗袜
她回到房内
放下水晶帘
静静遥望
那玲珑的秋月

【品读】

李白的这首小诗,设色是这般淡雅,就像那阶前缒立远视的少女……

玉阶、罗袜、水晶帘,居处的典丽与衣饰的幽雅,暗示着诗中人物品格的高华脱俗。

而在那月白风清的秋夜,为什么她要久久伫立?

她在等待,期盼什么?

抑或她在梦想,思忆着什么?

她奇特的美丽、未曾明言的忧伤,浸湿了我们的心。

让我想起佩特在《文艺复兴》中关于《蒙娜·丽莎》的那段文字:"这个在水次冉冉升起的如此奇妙的幽魂,她的面容倾倒了众生,但她的眼睑对此已透出厌倦。这是一种用奇思妙想和瑰丽的激情,塑造出来的美。能够用外在的形式提炼和表现出来的人世的所有思想和体验,都铭刻和熔铸在这张脸上。"

"在《蒙娜·丽莎》的画像中,佩特先生放进了一些列奥纳多做梦也没有想过的东西,可是谁在乎呢?"王尔德如是说。

说得多好啊,在这首小诗中,若是我读出了一些李白做梦也没有想过的东西,那又如何呢?

阅读,不正是开启自己与丰富作品吗?

杜甫（四首）

绝句

江碧鸟逾白，山青花欲燃。
今春看又过，何日是归年。

Quatrain

Against the blue mounts
And green river
The birds appear more white
the flowers seem even to blaze
The spring end is coming
When shall I go home

【诗绎】

映衬着碧绿的江水
鸟儿看上去更显洁白
青翠的山间红红的花儿
像要燃烧起来
这个春天又要过去了
哪一天才是我回乡的日子

【品读】

春天的美丽景色带给世人的不是慰藉而是更浓烈的乡愁。

在山间燃烧的是花的火焰,而在诗人心间燃烧着的则是一团乡愁的火焰,什么时候才能重返家园?

"月是故乡明",在另一首诗里,诗人这样表述自己对故乡的眷恋——这是带有几分偏执的爱。

王夫之《夕堂永日绪论》中说:"'青青河畔草',与'绵绵思远道',何以相因依,相含吐?神理凑合时,自然恰得。"

所有真正的生活是"相遇"(All the real living is meeting.),当人与自然相遇时顷,诗意遂于焉而生。

绝句

两个黄鹂鸣翠柳，一行白鹭上青天。
窗含西岭千秋雪，门泊东吴万里船。

Quatrain

Two yellow orioles are singing
amid the green willows
A flock of white egrets are flying
against the blue sky
The snow crowning western mountain
glows my window
Whilst, sails say
to my gate "Good bye"

【诗绎】

黄鹂在碧绿的柳叶间鸣唱
白鹭在蔚蓝的天空下飞翔
窗外西岭的白雪消泯了时间
门旁停泊的客船诉说着遥远

【品读】

黄、翠、青、白,诗人用文字的彩笔点染着春天的妩媚。而山巅永恒的白雪和江畔远行万里的航船又为这幅画卷平添一分哲思与壮美。

"千秋雪",是时间;"万里船",则是空间。而中文里,"间"是门隙透过的一缕月光,那么,在时"间"与空"间"中又流变生成着什么?是诗!是的,诗,在一个个"间"中流变生成,并借由"间"去颠覆一切固有的陈规成俗,让生命的意趣流逸如月光。

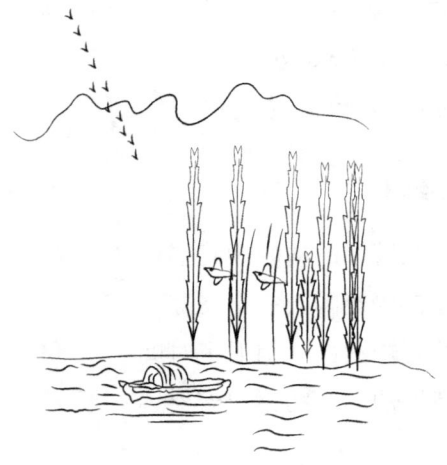

月夜

今夜鄜州月,闺中只独看。

遥怜小儿女,未解忆长安。

香雾云鬟湿,清辉玉臂寒。

何时倚虚幌,双照泪痕干。

On a Moonlight Night

Far off in Fuzhou
she watches the lonely moon
Alone from the window of her chamber
for our children
Poor little babes are too young to know
where the Capital is
Her cloudy hair is sweet with mist
Her jade-white shoulder is cold
in the moonlight
...when shall we get together again
with no more tears
Watching this bright moon on our screen?

【诗绎】

孩子们

还不懂得思念

今夜你在鄜州

只能独看

一片月色如霜

雾湿云鬟

光寒玉臂

什么时候 我们才能

在薄帏中偎依

望着那皎洁的月光

不再泪水盈盈

【品读】

月夜，诗人用思念的彩笔为远方的妻子绘就了一幅闺中念远图。

多少柔情多少牵挂多少辛酸啊。却是那样矜持节制。

全诗充盈着一种哀而不伤的古典美。

江南逢李龟年

岐王宅里寻常见，崔九堂前几度闻。
正是江南好风景，落花时节又逢君。

A Wandering Musician

*So often in Prince Qi's mansions
we did get together
Sometimes in the Cui's I heard you sing
Now we meet again
on the south of the Yangtze River
at the most beautiful time of year;
a parting spring with flowers falling*

【诗绎】

我的老友 你可记得

岐王宅里 崔九堂前

我们青春欢快的时辰

如今 时空转换

我们重逢在江南

而年华老去一如落花飘零

【品读】

友朋间的聚、散、离、合，是人世间的常情常态，敏感睿智的诗人却从中读出了时代的盛衰、家国的兴亡。

"正是江南好风景，落花时节又逢君。"飘零的落花，漂泊的身世，飘远的往昔，在难以抗拒的命运面前，诗人和音乐家只是留下高贵的泪水，默默承受一切，将自己沉溺于记忆任记忆的浪涛淹没自己。

于是，李龟年，这位流落江南的宫廷乐师，在杜甫笔下成为那个华丽而苍凉的时代的象征。

刘长卿（四首）

秋日登吴公台上寺远眺

古台摇落后， 秋入望乡心。
野寺人来少， 云峰水隔深。
夕阳依旧垒， 寒磬满空林。
惆怅南朝事， 长江独至今。

Autumn: A View on the Terrace

So autumn breaks my homesick heart
Few pilgrims venture climbing
to a temple so wild
Up from the lake
in the mountain clouds
sunset clings in the ancient defence
A stone gong shivers
through the empty woods
of the Southern Dynasty
What remains
Nothing but the great River

【诗绎】

秋日里的乡愁
如古台上草木的摇落
云峰深锁 水声悠远
荒凉的寺院人迹罕至
旧垒边夕阳依依
疏林中磬声清泠
江水流去南朝
往事多少惆怅

【品读】

在现世漂泊的诗人,他的心得以维系的却往往是另一个特定的时空。杜甫、大历七才子,就在乱世的风烟中重新发现了南朝那湮没于淫猥中的美。

巴赫金告诉我们,时空交汇的定点往往是叙述动机的发源地。在这首怀古诗中,诗人在现实、遐想与历史间微妙的互动中熔铸清丽悠远的情境,引人无限低回。

"惆怅南朝事,长江独至今。"在中原之外的南方,有着自己属于正统之外的传奇,那滔滔不尽的瑰伟与哀伤,那绵绵不已的乌托邦想象连接着屈子的汨罗、渊明的桃源,亦沾溉着一代代诗心。

送灵澈上人

苍苍竹林寺，杳杳钟声晚。
荷笠带夕阳，青山独归远。

Seeing off a Recluse

Green and green
The temple among bamboos
Ring and ring
The evening bell goes
Alas, my friend
while sunset fills your hat
I see you lost
in the blue hills

【诗绎】

青青的
竹林寺
钟声杳杳向晚
夕阳的余晖
盈满斗笠
你一个人
走向远山

【品读】

"苍苍""杳杳",叠声词的巧妙运用,让我们仿佛听到竹林寺悠远的钟声,应和着隐者的脚步,在那遥远静谧的黄昏回响。

是的,在那个黄昏,诗人站在石径上,目送着远去的背影,任钟声叩响心扉……

而时光就在那一刻停驶,诗亦在那一刻生成。

那是刹那的永恒?还是永恒的刹那?

俄国诗人、小说家蒲宁在小说《寒秋》的结尾中说:

我总是问自己:我一生中有过什么吗?我回答自己:有过的,只有过一件东西,就是那个寒秋的夜晚。

我想,那以美以真以善凝成的一瞬汇聚了人生所有的意义,剩下的时间不过是多余的梦而已。

不是吗?

逢雪宿芙蓉山主人

日暮苍山远,天寒白屋贫。
柴门闻犬吠,风雪夜归人。

Staying in Lotus Hill on a Snowy Night

Its sunset and the grey mount seems far
Cold and deserted the cottages are
At the gate a dog barks
With wind and snow
I come when it's dark

【诗绎】

黄昏
苍白的山
愈发淡远
清贫的小屋前
狗吠叫着寒冷
今夜,我和风和雪
一同叩响你的门扉

【品读】

天色向晚。

风,吹来片片雪意;犬,吠着声声寒冷。

诗人的这一首《逢雪宿芙蓉山主人》,是一段经历的自叙。简约、凝练的诗风,一如诗中那重白雪,覆盖了现实人生中的所有清苦与孤寂。

我觉得,读一首美丽的诗,宛若领受造物最神奇的赐予。不,一首美丽的诗,简直同造物一样神奇。

不是吗?那原本简单的文字,一旦进入诗,就可以抗拒时间的侵蚀,予我们以永远的感动。

布莱克在诗中说:

那是怎样的一双手啊/创造了猛虎/也创造了羔羊?

读完刘长卿的这首小诗,我想知道,又是怎样的一双手写出如此美妙的诗句?

听弹琴

泠泠七弦上,静听松风寒。
古调虽自爱,今人多不弹。

On Hearing a Lute Player

Your seven strings sound
of cold wind in the pines
Oh, sing old beloved songs
which no one cares for any more

【诗绎】

清泠的琴声
拂过琴弦
风
在松林间
回旋
我自爱这曲调的古朴
纵今人已不再弹它

【品读】

古罗马哲人西塞罗说:

Errare, mehercule, malo cum Platone, quam cumistis sentire. [我宁愿与柏拉图一起犯错,也不愿同那伙人(指毕达哥拉斯学派)一起正确。](Disput卷一)

同哲人、思者相比,诗人对信仰的执着,有过之而无不及。

换言之,诗人、思者不仅俱是不屑于趋奉的素心人,亦皆是荒寒路上的旅人。

因对真我的坚持而赢来的寂寥对于他们而言,不是困窘,而是一种高贵的自觉的选择。

韦应物（二首）

滁州西涧

独怜幽草涧边生，上有黄鹂深树鸣。
春潮带雨晚来急，野渡无人舟自横。

West Brook at Chuzhou

At dusk I walk alone by the brook
Here and there the green grass
a feast to my eyes
While listening to the songs
of the orioles up in the trees
The spring tide with heavy showers
comes hand in hand
A lonely boat is drifting
at the deserted crossing

【诗绎】

独步涧边幽草萋萋
树影深深鹂声离离
看春雨丰满了晚潮
孤舟横对渡口的荒凉

【品读】

诗是在诗中产生的(A poem grows out of poetry)。

《滁州西涧》作为韦应物的代表作,不仅鲜明地体现了韦诗特有的幽邃与古淡,而且孳乳了无数后人。

宋初苏舜钦那首《淮中晚泊犊头》,可谓承继演化此诗的一个范例:

春阴垂野草青青,时有幽花一树明。

晚泊孤舟古祠下,满川风雨看潮生。

再如王渔洋的《题野渡庵》:

西涧潇潇数骑过,韦公诗句奈愁何。

黄鹂唤客且须住,野渡庵前风雨多。

"满川风雨看潮生","野渡庵前风雨多",感动诗人与读者的是风雨中对美的执念。

秋夜寄丘员外

怀君属秋夜,散步咏凉天。
空山松子落,幽人应未眠。

Lines on an Autumn Night

The autumn night is so quiet
I walk along the trail
Missing you very much
Only the sound
of a tiny pine cone dropping
can you hear
in the secluded mount
Dear friend
You must be awake at this time
thinking of days
when we were together

【诗绎】

秋天的夜里
独自徘徊
我默默地想起
想起往昔我们一起
一起吟诵歌咏清凉的诗句
空山中松子 悄然落下
幽居的你 是否一样无眠
默默地想起
想起往昔我们一起
一起吟诵歌咏清凉的诗句

【品读】

韦应物的诗是那样静谧,静谧得像空旷的山,像林间悄然落下的松子。

"山空松子落",小巧的松子、偌大的山,两者的并置是有些略呈突兀,但突兀中却又别饶诗意。让人想起Wallace Stenvens 的名句"I placed a jar in Tennessee."(我放一只坛在田纳西)。

艺术的特质就是:它是为使感受摆脱习套而创作的,而创作者的目的是为提供一种视界,一种通过摆脱了习套的感受而获得的视界。(We find everywhere the artistic trademark—that is, we find material obviously created to remove the automatism of perception, the author's purpose is to create the vision which results from that deautomatized perception.—Victor Shklovesky "Art as Technique")

培根说:"读诗使人灵秀。"其原因或即在此。

张继(一首)

枫桥夜泊

月落乌啼霜满天,江枫渔火对愁眠。
姑苏城外寒山寺,夜半钟声到客船。

An Evening Song at Maple Bridge

The moon setting
The crows cawing
Frost spreads out against the sky
Maple trees on the bank
The dim lights from the fishing boats
And me with a sleepless midnight
From the Cold Mount Temple outside Gusu
ring bells and another sampan comes in

【诗绎】

月落 乌啼
繁霜满天
夜半 无眠的我
独对着江枫渔火
任寒山寺的钟声
叩打我的无眠

【品读】

这是中国诗歌史上最美丽的失眠。

一次落第成就了一首千古绝唱,生命中的得与失该如何衡量?是否赢得永恒 就意味着此世要将心酸与苦涩奉献给寒夜?

诗人能否走进历史的记忆,能否摆脱时间的侵蚀,不在于写得多,而在于是否写出锐利的诗行,洞穿岁月的铠甲。

司空曙(一首)

江村即事

钓罢归来不系船,江村月落正堪眠。
纵然一夜风吹去,只在芦花浅水边。

A Scene in a Riverside Village

Back from a fishing trip
There is no need to tie up the boat
The moon is down
It's time to sleep
If a night wind should blow the boat away
we'd still be in shallow waters
by the flowering reeds

【诗绎】

夜钓归来时候
江月斜照村头
不必系船了就这样睡吧
纵然夜风把船儿吹走
醒来后
还是一片浅水芦花

【品读】

诗人没有着力刻画江村的静谧恬美,但诗人幽雅悠闲的生活情趣已跃然纸上。

不知为什么,这首诗总让我想起朦胧诗人顾城那首《风偷走了我们的桨》:

就是这样/一阵风,温和地/偷走了我们的桨/墨绿色的湖水,玩笑地闪光"走吧,别再找了/再找出发的地方"/也许,夏雨的快乐使水闸塌方/在隐没的柳梢上/青蛙正指挥着一家练习合唱/也许,秋风吹干了云朵/大胆的蚂蚁正爬在干荷叶的帐篷上眺望/也许,一排年老的木桩还站在水里和小孩一起/等着小鱼把干净的玻璃瓶在青草中安放……

对简单、恬静的向往是今古相通的。

耿湋（一首）

秋日

反照入闾巷，忧来谁与语。
古道无人行，秋风动禾黍。

One Day in the Fall

The sunset moves over lanes
Who can sadness talk to?
The ancient road is little taken now
On wheat and corn fields
autumn winds blow

【诗绎】

夕阳返照着小巷
古道上几乎没有行人
秋风阵阵
吹动田间的禾黍
忧愁向谁诉

【品读】

诗人没有告诉我们他自己为什么忧愁,他自己的忧愁有多深。也许忧愁就像巷口的斜阳、禾黍上的秋风,自自然然地来了、去了,没办法也没必要说。

也许是这忧愁太遥远亦太久远:

行迈靡靡,中心摇摇,知我者,谓我心忧,不知我者,谓我何求,悠悠苍天,此何人哉!——《诗经·王风·黍离》

有谁能确定是谁最先唱起这首歌?但《秋日》中分明有着它的回音。

忧伤的歌者,尘世虽湮灭了你生命的印迹,但却无从阻碍你的歌声穿透漫漫世纪,在敏感的心间激荡,成为一个民族共有的记忆……

李益(二首)

江南曲

嫁得瞿塘贾,朝朝误妾期。
早知潮有信,嫁与弄潮儿。

A Complaint of Love

How many times
I have been disappointed by you
The busy merchant of Qutang
since we got married
Had I known the tide always
Keeps its word to come
I would have married a young tide-rider

【诗绎】

自从嫁给这个终朝忙碌的瞿塘商人
我就嫁给了等待与失望
早知道潮起潮落这样守时
我就该嫁给那弄潮的年青人

【品读】

江南,是地域的,更是文化的。那里有最美的人,最美的风景。

江南少许地,年年情不穷。江南虽小,却充盈着精致幽微、深情蜜意。诗中的女子像是从《西洲曲》中走来。"忆梅下西洲,折梅寄江北。单衫杏子红,双鬓鸦雏色。西洲在何处?西桨桥头渡。日暮伯劳飞,风吹乌臼树。树下即门前,门中露翠钿。开门郎不至,出门采红莲。采莲南塘秋,莲花过人头。低头弄莲子,莲子清如水。置莲怀袖中,莲心彻底红。忆郎郎不至,仰首望飞鸿。鸿飞满西洲,望郎上青楼。楼高望不见,尽日栏杆头。栏杆十二曲,垂手明如玉。卷帘天自高,海水摇空绿。海水梦悠悠,君愁我亦愁。南风知我意,吹梦到西洲。"

她的埋怨也是那么娇憨、纯情,让人听来不禁哑然失笑。

夜上受降城闻笛

回乐烽前沙似雪,受降城外月如霜。
不知何处吹芦管,一夜征人尽望乡。

On Hearing a Reed Flute

The sand around the ramparts
streams like snow
... the moon looks like frost
beyond the city wall
Someone is playing
a reed flute
making the soldiers
think of home all night long

【诗绎】

回乐烽前
受降城外
月色如霜
沙漠如雪
谁人何处
一声芦管
已让今夜
尽染乡愁

【品读】

回乐烽前,受降城外,"沙似雪""月如霜",一俯视、一仰视,俯仰之间,上下交映,但觉白光一片,寒意浸人,而悠扬的芦管,则使整首诗由孤迥的空间转向瞬息零落的时间,在戍边将士的心头又平添几分寂寞。此际,谁会不想家呢?

那声芦管,就像普鲁斯特(Proust)笔下的玛德琳娜小糕点,马丁村教堂尖塔变幻的阴影,不其然地唤醒了心底沉睡的记忆。

记忆里悠扬的该是笛声、箫音。那么,声声芦管,提示的只是故乡的失落——故乡只能在心底,在遥望中。

诗人没有说乡愁有多沉重,一切都呈现在那自身具足的意象之中。

孟郊（一首）

游子吟

慈母手中线，游子身上衣。

临行密密缝，意恐迟迟归。

谁言寸草心，报得三春晖。

Mother Love

Needle and thread in hand
The mother sews the clothes
stitch by stitch for her son
who is going to roam
Afraid is she
that he will prolong his journey away
from home
for this reason
or that
As the saying goes
Mother's love is to her children
what the spring sun is to grass
What should we do to return her devotion

【诗绎】

慈爱的母亲

为远行的游子

缝制了衣衫

那细密的针脚

是不尽的叮咛

千万不要延误了归期

小草如何回报三月的暖阳

游子又拿什么献给他挚爱的母亲

【品读】

母爱是静谧深邃的,像清泉默默滋养着你……而你也许并不经意,直到有一天,远在天涯的你,想起故乡那为岁月压弯了的倚间望归的身影,才悄悄流下泪珠两颗。

这是对母爱的报答?!

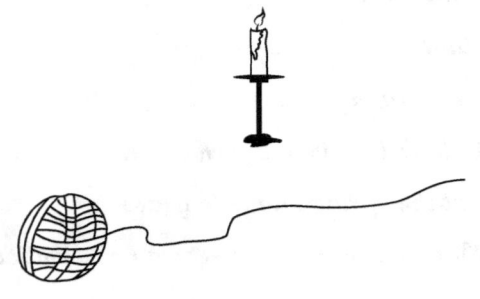

韩愈（二首）

早春呈水部张十八员外

天街小雨润如酥，草色遥看近却无。
最是一年春好处，绝胜烟柳满皇都。

Early Spring

On the royal street
the fine rain is as soft as cream
There grass is like mist
more felt than seen
It's the best time of year
far better than late spring
when the capital is veiled with willows

【诗绎】

街头小雨柔润如酥
一痕草色若有若无
知否此际春光最美
远胜满城柳烟迟暮

【品读】

还记得自己怎样在细雨中走过早春的街头吗？那抹翠盈盈的绿意，是生机，是希望，宛若透明的雾给我们多少清新的喜悦。

静静的品味这首小诗，我们的心将为诗人对美的渴求、向往与坚持而悸动。在平淡无奇的日常生活中竟也蕴有如此精致、细微的美？如果我们有诗人对美的敏感，不，也许更准确地说，该是对美的信仰，那么，我们在这丑陋的俗世也能建起美的乐园。

美，是对陈俗的超越。

美，是用心去叩问宇宙的苍莽。

美，是另一种宗教，
信仰它，永恒的女神，
将引领我们飞升！

晚春

草树知春不久归,百般红紫斗芳菲。
杨花榆荚无才思,惟解漫天作雪飞。、

Late Spring

Flowers and blossoms know
spring will leave soon
Thus, they do manage to show their best
Ordinary as the willow catkins are
they still learn to fly
here and there like snow

【诗绎】

知道春天就要离开
花与树争现着最后的美
纵然是柳絮榆荚
也像雪一样飘飞

【品读】

青山自青山,白云自白云,以物观物,而不以身观物,那是哲人。在诗人眼里,万物有情。于是,即将离去的春天、绽放的花树与飘舞的柳絮榆荚,无论瑰奇平凡,仿佛在一同举办一场美的华宴。那是辞行,更是相约吧?

济慈在信中曾经说过:美是无上的,它克制、湮灭其他的应考虑的事物。

那什么又是"应考虑的事物"?是现实中那些有价的、可以计算的利害关系,是生命中务实、功利的维度。

而真正的诗人,作为美的服膺者,却对那"应考虑的事物"总是视若无睹。

他们只注目于宇宙的大美。那纵使殒落也一样让人心悸的美!

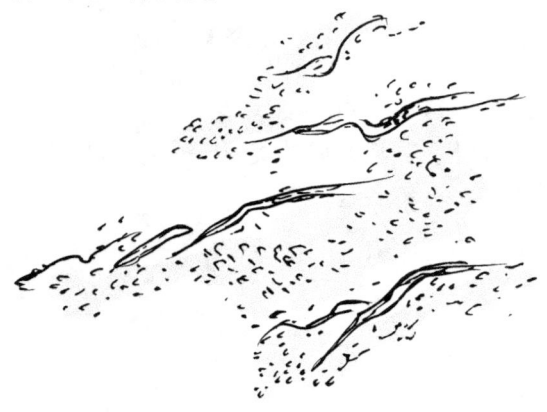

柳宗元(二首)

江雪

千山鸟飞绝，万径人踪灭。
孤舟蓑笠翁，独钓寒江雪。

Snow

Beyond mountains and mountains
There is no bird
but snow
Along paths and paths
there is no traveler
but snow
Only on a freezing river
there is a fisherman
alone, old
He is fishing nothing
but snow

【诗绎】

山中看不见飞鸟的痕迹

路上找不到前行的脚印

天地间 只有雪和雪一般的寂静

而那穿着蓑衣戴着笠帽的渔翁

却守着一叶孤舟

在寒江上独自垂钓

【品读】

没有了喧闹的鸟鸣,没有了奔忙的人群,诗人用"绝""灭""孤""独"四字呈现出一个清冷孤寂的世界——是现世也是内心。

渔父是中国诗歌中一个颇具象征意味的原型。他是终日垂钓钓人主的英雄;他是狷介不苟的隐士,"沧浪之水清兮,可以濯吾缨;沧浪之水浊兮,可以濯吾足";他是喧嚣的世界中默默以存的智者,"屈原既放,游于江潭,行吟泽畔,颜色憔悴,形容枯槁",这生命的逐客对着"深思高举"的三闾大夫却只悠悠地说:"世人皆浊,何不淈其泥而扬其波?众人皆醉,何不哺其糟而歠其醨?"

道路修远,桃源已逝,再没有人主,也没有诗人,渔父只能独钓江雪独钓孤独。

渔翁

渔翁夜傍西岩宿，晓汲清湘燃楚竹。
烟销日出不见人，欸乃一声山水绿。
回看天际下中流，岩上无心云相逐。

The Aged Fisherman

In the night
an aged fisherman puts himself up
by the western cliffs
At dawn, he fetches water
from the clear Xiang
And makes a bamboo fire
only then, the sunrise finds him
Disappearing with the mist
Only the sound of his oar echoes
in the greenness of mountain and river
Now, look around and you'll see
the waves rolling from heaven
and one cloud after another
coming and going idly over the cliffs

【诗绎】

夜晚 渔翁的船泊在西面的山崖下

黎明 他汲引清澈的湘水 点燃楚竹

然后 当朝岚散去

白亮亮的太阳升起

我们却再看不到他的身影

只听到青山绿水间欸乃的歌声在回荡

江流汤汤 奔向天际

山岩上 白云不经意地飘着

【品读】

清人贺裳《载酒园诗话》论韦、柳诗风异同云："韦、柳相同者，神骨之清；相异者，不独峭淡之分，先自忧乐之别"，以此诗与韦应物名作《滁州西涧》对读，可见贺之灼见。

而宋代大诗人苏轼认为，把最后两句删掉，整首诗会更有韵味，更美。

信然。

崔护(一首)

题都城南庄

去年今日此门中,人面桃花相映红。
人面不知何处去,桃花依旧笑春风。

Last Year

A year ago today we meet in the villa
Her pretty face
and peach blossoms
glowed each other
Now she is in another place—
Nobody knows where
Only the peach blossoms are left to smile
in the spring breeze

【诗绎】

今日的柴扉深锁着昨天的记忆
——青春的娇羞映衬着桃花的俏丽
而你在哪里?
春风桃李间我感受着你的气息

【品读】

只是一次偶遇。只有长长的留白。没有故事。

像埃兹拉·庞德(Ezra Pound)的 In a Station of the Metro（《在一个地铁车站》）："The apparition of these faces in the crowd;Petals on a wet, black bough."（众中面影幻丽，黝湿枝条疏花。）生命中，美的呈现(presence)与消失(absence)不就是这样猝然？未及回首，已成过往。

生命本来的样貌，一旦入诗，却美得让人窒息。

王建(一首)

望夫石

望夫处,江悠悠。化为石,不回头。
山头日日风复雨,行人归来石应语。

Petrified

Where she waits for her husband
the river rolls forever
She's turned into a rock
and still stands on the hill
day in and day out
Against the wind and rain.
When the husband returns some day
the rock-wife will come back to life
Telling him
what has happened to her

【诗绎】

江流依旧
我化为山头的礁石
承受着岁月的风雨
却没有改变遥望的身姿
啊,远行的人,待你归来
我会悄悄对你诉说这等待的日夜

【品读】

"候人兮猗!"——史书中铭刻的只是那女子的一声喟叹,一声没有应答的呼唤,映衬着禹远去的步履。

从此,等待与寂寥成为女子的专利,而当她成为诗,成为石,成为传奇,复有几人能读出其中的凄楚?

成为诗,成为石,这是父权制中女子的宿命,说诗人却只蛊惑于承诺的美与真!

刘禹锡（三首）

竹枝词

杨柳青青江水平，闻郎江上唱歌声。
东边日出西边雨，道是无晴却有晴。

The Bamboo Song

The willows are green
The river levels with the banks
Your songs float across the ripping water
To the east it is sunny
To the west it is rainy
Could you tell me whether it shines or rains?

【诗绎】

岸上的绿柳
轻拂着江面
远远传来你的歌声
似在倾诉又像问询：
东边柔柔的日光
西边细细的雨丝
你可知那是无晴还是有晴

【品读】

"东边日出西边雨,道是无晴却有晴",所以有阳光与阴雨的组接,不正是因为爱中的明媚与哀伤同在?

我想起《越人歌》:"今夕何夕兮,搴舟中流。今日何日兮,得与王子同舟。蒙羞被好兮,不訾诟耻。心几烦而不绝兮,得知王子。山有木兮木有枝(知),心悦君兮君不知。" 虽然,《竹枝词》中的女孩似乎没有恁多哀愁,但作为思慕者,心是一样谦卑的。

张纲孙评清真词:"结构天成,而中有艳语、隽语、奇语、豪语、苦语、痴语、没要紧语,如巧匠运斤,毫无痕迹。"(冯煦《宋六十一家词选例言》引)

刘禹锡的《竹枝词》,亦涵容着众多的异质成分。设若将"道是无晴却有晴"理解为歌中女孩慧黠的答语,整首诗将是另一种气象。

石头城

山围故国周遭在,潮打空城寂寞回。
淮水东边旧时月,夜深还过女墙来。

The Stone City

The winding hills embrace the ancient capital
The rolling waves beat on its ruined walls
With the river's tide uprises the moon bright
And at midnight the city overflows her light

【诗绎】

青山无语 环拥着故都
江潮寂寞 轻叩着城墙
月上中天一如从前
只默默地默默地注视
自己的清影

【品读】

"怀古"者,见古迹,思古人,其事无他,兴亡贤愚而已。可以为法而不之法,可以为戒而不之戒,则又以悲夫后之人也。齐彭殇之修短,忘尧桀之是非,则异端之说也。有仁心者必为世道计,故不能自默于斯焉。

方回认为诗人应在怀古中寄寓兴亡之感,而不是简单地为荒台、废园这类"缺失的景象"伤感。

但规避道德评价却往往赋予这类诗更大的艺术魅力。本诗的优长就在于诗人将所有的感慨感叹都隐去了,给予读者的是空,是留白,是无尽的遐思。

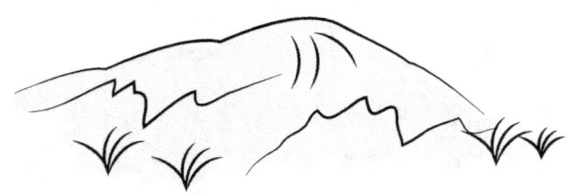

乌衣巷

朱雀桥边野草花,乌衣巷口夕阳斜。
旧时王谢堂前燕,飞入寻常百姓家。

Black Robe Lane

By the Red Sparrow Bridge
flowers and grasses grow
over Black Robe Lane
The setting sun is hanging low
Alas the dusk finds swallows
flying to nest in the humble homes
that used to be the grand halls

【诗绎】

朱雀桥边的野花
明媚着今朝的美丽
乌衣巷口的斜阳
凄切着过往的记忆
主人变了堂前的春燕
依旧飞入熟悉的旧巢

【品读】

在人世与自然的对照中,我们懂得了生命的脆弱与尊严。它铭刻着历史的风华,也承载着时间的衰颜。

这首怀古诗,今天读来,让我们感动的已经不是对前朝的凭吊,而是对生命摧折的叹惋。

元稹(一首)

行宫

寥落古行宫,宫花寂寞红。
白头宫女在,闲坐说玄宗。

At a Summer Palace

At a deserted Summer Palace
the flowers still blooms
The white-haired palace ladies
talk about the good old days
At leisure

【诗绎】

旧日的行宫那般寥落
宫中的花儿也红得寂寞
满头白发的宫女们
闲坐絮语着往昔

【品读】

诗中弥漫的是一种挽歌的情调。

那曾经美轮美奂的行宫，已成为寥落的荒园；而那曾经婀娜妩媚的宫女，也已成为白发苍苍的老妪。

"曾经"也许是世上最残酷的一个词，试想有多少美与崇高在其间萎落成泥？

"曾经"是隐性的柔和的死亡，是一个世界的坠落与缺席。

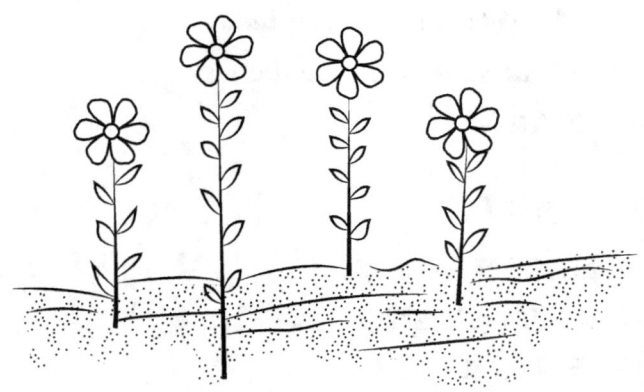

白居易(三首)

赋得古原草送别

离离原上草,一岁一枯荣。
野火烧不尽,春风吹又生。
远芳侵古道,晴翠接荒城。
又送王孙去,萋萋满别情。

Grass on Ancient Plain

The grass grows
nice and thick on the Plain
Year after year
it turns yellow and green
Bushfires cannot wipe it out
Spring breeze causes it to come to life
It overgrows along the ancient path
and reaches as far as the deserted city
Though we part with each other
it will accompany you
with my love forever

【诗绎】

古原青草离离

年年岁岁 枯枯荣荣

野火从未将她烧尽

春风又来把她唤醒

绵绵古道

悠悠荒城

都写满她的身影

满载我的别情

伴你远行

【品读】

"王孙游兮不归,春草生兮萋萋",从《楚辞·招隐士》起,草与离情在中国古典诗歌中就绾结在了一起。芳草天涯,思念也同样的绵远。

暮江吟

一道残阳铺水中,半江瑟瑟半江红。
可怜九月初三夜,露似真珠月似弓。

The Twilight River

The setting sun spreads its light
against the skies
The river is a flowing jade
Dark green and deep red
how lovely it is tonight!
The dewdrops are pearls
And the moon is a bow

【诗绎】

江面是流动的画卷
夕阳的画笔
涂抹着深深浅浅的碧与红
多美啊九月初三的夜晚
秋露如珠新月如弓

【品读】

印象派画家Sisley雅好寥廓的长天,他说:"天空以她绵延不尽的层次给画面以深度和动感。"(Not only does it give the picture depth through its successive planes, it also gives movement.)

而另一位印象派大师Monet则钟爱着水钟爱着离合的波光钟爱着清奇的涟漪钟爱着水中光影交汇与交错的镜像。

我想,如果诗人与两位画家在天国相遇,他们之间一定有良好的互动。

不是吗?夕阳、晚霞、新月、秋露、暮江,像Monet、Sisley一样,诗人用光与影为我们书写了一页如画的诗章。

问刘十九

绿蚁新醅酒,红泥小火炉。
晚来天欲雪,能饮一杯无?

Asking a Friend

It's evening, and looks like snowing
Do come and drink together
You know green wine is warming on
a tiny red clay stove

【诗绎】

新酿的米酒 还未过滤
红泥小炉里 炉火正旺
天黑了 要落雪
来共饮一杯吧?

【品读】

酿雪的黄昏,淡淡的邀约。白居易与刘轲的小聚成就了中国诗史上一个温暖的瞬间。

乐天的诗,像日记,絮絮地书写着自己的欢喜、悲情。欢喜时,恨不能拥抱万物,"回头问双石,能伴老夫否。石虽不能言,许我为三友";悲情时,又感伤得要死,"天长地久有时尽,此恨绵绵无绝期";高傲时,目无余子,"唐兴二百年,其间诗人不可胜数。所可举者,陈子昂有《感遇诗》二十首,鲍防《感兴诗》十五篇。又诗之豪者,世称李、杜。李之作,才矣!奇矣!人不逮矣!索其风雅比兴,十无一焉。杜诗最多,可传者千余首。至于贯穿古今,尔见缕格律,尽工尽善,又过于李焉。然撮其《新安》《石壕》《潼关吏》《芦子关》《花门》之章,'朱门酒肉臭,路有冻死骨'之句,亦不过十三四";谦逊起来会过度自卑,热情时,要熔融世界;冷漠起来,又那样枯槁,坚强时,傲视一切命运的播弄;懦弱时,却又那样避风避雨战战兢兢。

诚然,他的诗,并非篇篇可诵。有的甚或鄙俚、质直。

但他的创造力,却永远充沛着、闪耀着,像大自然深邃而原始的力。

李贺(一首)

苏小小墓

幽兰露,如啼眼。
无物结同心,烟花不堪剪。
草如茵,松如盖。风为裳,水为珮。
油壁车,夕相待。冷翠烛,劳光彩。
西陵下,风吹雨。

Sue, a late Singing Girl

Like a violet
Half hidden from the eye
The dewdrops are her tears
when she walks by the grass
Under the pines her dress
Flows in the breeze
Her jade shimmers like water
A Stead waiting in twilight
A candle glittering in vain
Winds chase
Rain chases
Winds
upon her grave

【诗绎】

你有露珠的泪
你有幽兰的哀伤
绿松为你遮阴
青草陪你远行
取风为裳
以水为佩
油壁车 在夕阳下 伫候
烛光也默默憔悴
只有雨滴轻轻轻轻 轻坠西陵

【品读】

李贺诗予人的审美感受是一种混合着惊奇与惊艳的"震惊"。如年轻的杜牧所言:

云烟绵联,不足为其态也;水之迢迢,不足为其情也;春之盎盎,不足为其和也;秋之明洁,不足为其格也;风樯阵马,不足为其勇也;瓦棺篆鼎,不足为其古也;时花美女,不足为其色也;荒国陊殿,梗莽丘陇,不足为其恨怨悲愁也;鲸呿鳌掷,牛鬼蛇神,不足为其虚荒诞幻也。

而这样矛盾的审美效果,源自于李贺文本特有的罅隙与空白:李贺写诗时,致力于每一诗句的完美,而每一完美的诗句也就各自成为一个世界,以致读者流连于某句诗时,却不知如何泅渡到下一诗行。

李贺的诗思凝成的是一个个结晶的句子,而不是浑融的诗篇。这是他歌诗的独特的美质与瑕疵。

薛涛(二首)

送友人

水国蒹葭夜有霜，月寒山色共苍苍。
谁言千里自今夕，离梦杳如关塞长。

Saying Adieu, Adieu, Adieu

In the water reeds
with rushes covered with frost
The moon's coldness
And the mountain cast solitude
They say you'll be
three hundred miles away
from tonight on
But my dreams of you won't leave
They'll accompany you
to the distant frontier

【诗绎】

今夜

秋霜落满了蒹葭

今夜

月光分享着山的苍凉

今夜

我的梦伴你远行塞上

【品读】

这是一首幽婉的月光装饰的骊歌,银白的霜里,萧疏的蒹葭轻轻地吟诵着,如铮、如瑟。

"蒹葭苍苍,白露为霜。所谓伊人,在水一方。"诗人互文的表达,设定了诗的情感流向,为等待与绝望画上了等号:等待是最漫长的绝望,绝望是最遥远的等待。

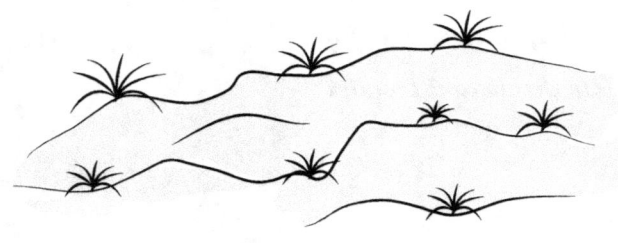

风

猎蕙微风远，飘弦唳一声。
林梢鸣淅沥，松径夜凄清。

Breeze

Seeking marsh orchids
A light breeze comes and goes
It flows over strings gently
Twigs in the woods
Sing in whistles and rustles
Along paths through the pine trees
night finds it walking
cool and fresh

【诗绎】

远远拂过清丽的兰草
轻轻叩响静默的琴弦
林梢雨声淅沥
夜色覆满松间那弯小径

【品读】

薛涛的诗像林间的那缕风,隽永、飘逸、空灵,又不胜清怨,让你无从揣测。

如伽达默尔所言,艺术乃是通过不确定性抵达了存在,它使存在是其所是,无限可能的是。

飘弦唳一声,要怎样的音声才可以称为"唳"?在薛涛的诗里,我们读到的是女性柔情与激情的造物。光与阴影都是那样浓重,可以铭于心、刻于骨。

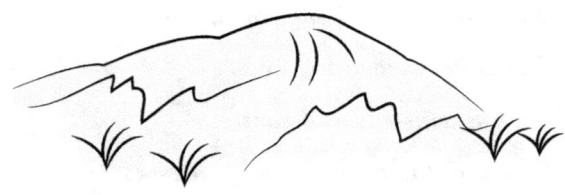

张祜（一首）

宫词

故国三千里，　深宫二十年。
一声何满子，　双泪落君前。

Palace Poem

A thousand miles from her homeland
Deep in the palace these twenty years
At the first sound of "Ho Man-tzu"
A pair of tears fall in front of her lord

【诗绎】

故国遥遥三千里
宫闱深深二十年
轻轻一声何满子
双泪洒落在君前

【品读】

注意到了吗？在这四句诗中每句都有一个数字，前两行中的数字很大，而后两行中的数字很小。

是的，年深日久的悲怆流出来也不过泪珠两颗。诗所蕴涵的强大的感情冲击力就在这样的对比中产生。

法国诗人马拉美认为，诗人应该让自己曾深入观察过的物象孤立起来，然后把它压缩成本身的真质，那具有暗示力的诗人与物象的微妙关系能够迫使读者用他从未有过的眼光去看那物象。

这首《宫词》不就有这样的审美效果吗？

杜牧(四首)

泊秦淮

烟笼寒水月笼沙,夜泊秦淮近酒家。
商女不知亡国恨,隔江犹唱后庭花。

A Mooring at Qinhuai River

Mist over cold water, moon over the sand on Qinhuai
near a restaurant our boat stands
The singing girls
across the River are humming
the Inner Court Flower
But, there is no sorrow
over loss of country to their tunes

【诗绎】

月光静静地流成了银色

雾像柔曼的轻纱

悄笼着一湾寒水

两岸白沙

今夜,秦淮

隔江的女子唱着《后庭花》

岁月洗去忧伤

【品读】

这首诗标志着中国诗史上一个重要的时刻。

从此,历代的读者都把秦淮的烟波与历史的盛衰联系了起来。桨声灯影中的那份惆怅从未老去。但在诗人忧伤、迷离的诗行里,那在江干曼声而歌的女子是否让我们想起那在水之湄的伊人?如是,拨动我的心弦的就不只是星移物化的鼎革迁逝,还有一种对遥远而又切近的美的企慕,那么淡远,那么隽永……

当,一首诗写下来,它或许完成了,却还没有终止;它在自己身上,在作者那里,在读者那里,在沉默中寻找另一首诗。

山行

远上寒山石径斜， 白云生处有人家。
停车坐爱枫林晚， 霜叶红于二月花。

Mountain Trip

The stone steps look long and steep
Several cloud-capped homes sit on the peak
It's autumn twilight and please
stop my carriage by the Maplewood
I like to watch its frost-touched leaves
As you see they turn
as red as Early Spring Delight

【诗绎】

石径 蜿蜒
白云生处
人家几户
斜阳下经霜的枫叶
红艳如花
只为这美景
我把车停了又停

【品读】

"寒山""石径""白云""霜叶",被诗人用惊喜的目光统摄起来,构成一幅秋山行旅图。

湛湛江水兮上有枫,自宋玉以降,诗歌中的枫总与某种愁情联系在一起。杜牧在《山行》中颠覆了这一套式。跃然纸上的是诗人高雅脱俗的情趣。

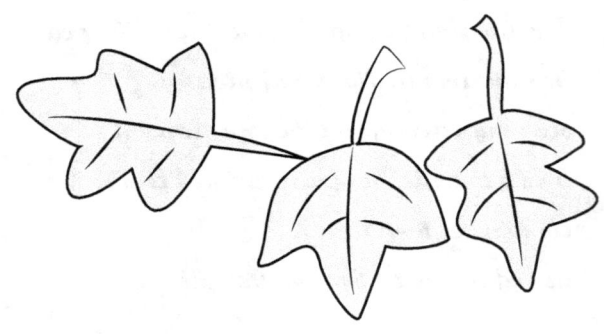

秋夕

银烛秋光冷画屏,轻罗小扇扑流萤。
天阶夜色凉如水,坐看牵牛织女星。

An Autumn Night

*A silvery candle
gives the painted screen
an icy light
on the autumn night
The girl in silk robe is using
a fan to catch fireflies
At this hour
the palace steps seem
as cold as water
She sits watching two stars
in love meet in skies*

【诗绎】

秋夜 流成水蓝
萤光迷离
银色的烛火 清冷了画屏
薄薄的罗衫
小小的团扇
她醉了
卧看牵牛织女天阶漫步

【品读】

美与寂寞的边界,许是比蛛丝还细的透明的线。因而,当我们为美感动时,不觉间也被寂寞浸染。

设若少女妆台间没有镜子/成天凝望悬在壁上的宫扇/扇上的楼阁如水中倒影/染着剩粉残泪如烟云……

这是何其芳为《画梦录》写下的序言。在同文中,这位总是为美与寂寞喟叹的少年诗人继续写道:"我倒是喜欢想象着一些辽远的东西。一些不存在的人物。和许多在人类的地图上找不出名字的国土。我说不清有多少日夜,像故事里所说的一样,对着壁上的画出神遂走入画里去了。但我的墙壁是白色的。不过那金色的门,那不知是乐园还是地狱的门,确曾为我开启过而已。"

想来,那"金色的门",该是泛义的诗的象喻,因为只有诗才能同时融汇神启与魔力。

诗中,杜牧通过少女的眼,将银烛、流萤与牵牛、织女并列在一起,是在隐喻青春虽像烛光、萤火一样短暂,美,却可以像星辰一样永恒。总之,以这样的并置,诗人将人世与自然乃至超自然之境化合为一,心灵与外物之间不复有界线存在。

或称诗人每每醉心于人生的表现,但在诗中,表现即内容。

赠别

多情却似总无情,唯觉尊前笑不成。
蜡烛有心还惜别,替人垂泪到天明。

A Parting Song

Sorrow is within myself
too deep to convey in words
Only during toasting
am I aware
I failed to smile
The candle seems
to sympathize with us
melting in tears
as our hearts do

【诗绎】

空白的心版沉淀了太多的思绪
往日的欢乐凝成樽前的沉寂
就让蜡烛为彼此布置一个别离的背景
今夜一点一点将心燃尽

【品读】

"一片伤心画不成。"是啊,该用怎样的色彩、线条去描摹心内的那份神伤的纹呢?

当画家不得不为之搁笔时,诗人却用传神的语言为我们传达了别离时那欲语还休、无以自拔的情致。

"蜡烛有心还惜别,替人垂泪到天明。"离人的情感转移到了蜡烛上,蜡烛在落泪,恍若它也分担了一分离情。

火销蚀了蜡烛,离情是否也会让我们消陨?

李商隐（四首）

霜月

初闻征雁已无蝉，百尺楼高水接天。
青女素娥俱耐冷，月中霜里斗婵娟。

Frost and Moon

When we hear first calls
of the wild geese
No more do cicadas sing
South of hundred-foot tower
water and sky merge into one
The Frost Beauty
and the Moon Lady
rivals in elegance
brave the cold together
now

【诗绎】

不再有

蝉声如雨

青冷的长空

唯有雁鸣

掠过

独上高楼

水天澄明

素月　银霜

具象莹白的美

【品读】

神话与诗，是人在这个被上帝抛弃的世界建构的属于自己的伊甸。

虽然没有"彼岸"的信仰，义山的诗思里却一样有着神话的丰厚积淀。

"山沓水匝，树杂云合。目既往还，心亦吐纳。春日迟迟，秋风飒飒。情往似赠，兴来如答。"（刘勰《文心雕龙·物色》）——华夏山水美学的浸润，则让诗人与自然之间的交流更体己更纯粹。

夜雨寄北

君问归期未有期,巴山夜雨涨秋池。
何当共剪西窗烛,却话巴山夜雨时。

A Rainy Night

You ask about my return
But I don't know
Here, the pond overflows
with the autumn rain on Mount Ba
Deep in the night
oh when can we trim the candle
By the western window
And talk about
what's happening tonight

【诗绎】

你问起归期
那串数不完的日子
我无语
巴山夜色如墨
洒下来盈满秋池
哦,待到你我重聚
共剪西窗烛花
我会静静告诉你
今夜的情境

【品读】

夜雨难眠,独对残烛,诗人一次次翻读友人询问归期的信笺,如何作复?所以憧憬重聚憧憬在重聚的欢乐中追怀今夜的种种,恰是因为现实的"今夜"不堪言说无从言说。

历史无情。当它记住一位诗人时,是因为诗人以美的力量刻写出生命的真。

乐游原

向晚意不适,驱车登古原。
夕阳无限好,只是近黄昏。

Grief at Dusk

At dusk my heart aches for some reason
So I drive my cab to the ancient plateau
The night is about to fall
The sinking sun shines splendid, though

【诗绎】

傍晚时候
心中莫名地难受
驾车来到乐游原上
看那朵夕阳
陨落的辉煌

【品读】

夕阳,将辉煌与陨落集于一身,古往今来,曾引来多少中外诗人、思者的凝眸。

叶燮《原诗·内篇》云:

诗之至处,妙在含蓄无垠,思致微渺。其寄托在可言不可言之间,其指归在可解不可解之会,言在此而意在彼,泯端倪而离形象,绝议论而穷思维,引人于冥漠恍惚之境,所以为至也。

又云:

幽渺以为理,想象以为事,惝恍以为情。

以之品鉴义山这首幽韵冷香的小诗,堪称的评。

嫦娥

云母屏风烛影深,长河渐落晓星沉。
嫦娥应悔偷灵药,碧海青天夜夜心。

Lady in the Moon

The candle light shimmers
Its faint shadow
sweeps over the screen
The heaven river is running dry
And the morning star fading out
You may regret—
the immortal poison should be fatal to you
Night by night
immerse yourself in a sea of solitude

【诗绎】

烛影摇曳

轻轻拂过一角

屏风

天河流尽　晨星隐映

此刻　你听凭悔意啃噬

——那不死的药竟是致命的毒

于是　夜　夜　夜　夜

你任一天如海的孤寂浸没自己

【品读】

这首《嫦娥》，不妨视作义山的alibi。

Alibi　作为法律名词意为"不在场证明"。但它还包含的另一层意思则是以不在场的方式言说自己的在场。即，置身另一个场域，却言说着此在的欣慨。

这不正是义山的写照？

蓬山梦杳，灵犀难通，在零落的生息中，也许唯有他笔下生成的嫦娥，才能抚慰他的焦灼。

在姮娥那一天如海的孤寂里，投影着义山自己的迷惘与忧伤。

温庭筠(一首)

瑶瑟怨

冰簟银床梦不成,碧天如水夜云轻。
雁声远过潇湘去,十二楼中月自明。

A Jade Lute

A mat on the silvery bed is cool like ice
when night sky appears
As green as water
With tender clouds flowing on it
But can you hear the calling of a
wild goose beyond Xiao and Xiang
And no dreams come to me
in the twelve-story building
Under the moon

【诗绎】

银床冰簟

碧天轻云

明月似水

征雁远去潇湘

十二楼中

锦瑟伴我

中宵无眠

【品读】

整首诗,是那么的清丽哀伤,宛然超越了具体的画图而步入了音乐的境界。读过之后,我们不知道也不在意真正发生了什么,感动我们的是那缥缈曼妙的情思。

杜威说:"人的世界是一个充满符号与象征的世界。"我想,若将这句话移来说诗也一样甚或更其准确。"冰簟""银床""雁声""月明",这些"符号"与"象征"唤醒了我们心底多少沉睡的诗意?

真该感谢诗人,他们会让哀愁也变得如此美丽。"寒山一带伤心碧","红楼隔雨相望冷",某天,当凄凉漫过心堤,请你轻轻吟哦这绝美的诗句,相信胸腹间那缕凄凉将袅袅飘散。

高骈(一首)

山亭夏日

绿树阴浓夏日长,楼台倒影入池塘。
水精帘动微风起,满架蔷薇一院香。

Green

Green
And greener
The summers day is ideal
among the trees
Fine buildings watch their own reflections
on the water
The crystal curtains stir
when a light breeze descends
A bed of rose envelopes
the garden with their scents

【诗绎】

悠长的夏日

绿树摇曳

美丽的楼台

倒影水中

微风起

水晶帘动

庭院里浸满

蔷薇的香氛

【品读】

这首诗用一个个精致的画面拼贴出一帧美丽的夏景。微风起处,水晶帘动,蔷薇的那缕暗香为我们留下风的体味。

诗中,现实的物象往往因诗人的杰思而有了一层幻美的光晕。

赵嘏(一首)

江楼感旧

独上江楼思渺然,月光如水水如天。
同来望月人何处,风景依稀似去年。

On the Passing Days

Lost in thought
I'm alone in the tower
Under my feet
the moon still glides along the river
Water and sky look one color
Oh, where are you now, my friends
Everything is the same as last year
But you left

【诗绎】

一个人
登上江楼
思绪渺然
月光如水
水如天
一样的是风景
不一样的是孤单

【品读】

人人都看的眼前景,个个都有的心中事,却只有他婉转清新地写成了一首诗。

真不明白柏拉图的理想国为什么要把诗人拒之门外。没有了诗,生命的景观该是多么平庸。

韦庄(一首)

台城

江雨霏霏江草齐,六朝如梦鸟空啼。
无情最是台城柳,依旧烟笼十里堤。

The City of Tai

A fine rain falls
on the grass along the river
Six dynasties are gone like a dream
The birds keep twittering in vain
Untouched, the willows envelope
the ten-mile-long bank
As ever
in the green mist

【诗绎】

细雨 蒙蒙
青草 依依
鸟喃喃呓语着 往事如梦
江畔的柳烟
轻笼长堤 依旧

【品读】

在台城，诗人凭吊古迹，回望六朝风烟。

沿着烟雨迷蒙的长堤，诗人仿佛步入了逝者的国度。

而那些已为时光黯淡了的名字，此刻，似乎又隐现于绿柳依依的深处……

如何不为历史埋没？当诗人嗟叹死亡时，他是在凝思生之意义。

韩偓（一首）

效崔国辅体

淡月照中庭，海棠花自落。
独立俯闲阶，风动秋千索。

In Cui's Manner

The pale moon shines on the mid-yard
Petals float down
from the crabapple's
She finds herself standing
alone on the steps
The swing sways in the breeze

【诗绎】

淡淡的月光洒满中庭
海棠花径自飘落
一个人站在阶前望着
秋千在微风里轻轻轻轻地摇

【品读】

塞尚说:"莫奈只是一双眼睛,而那是一双多么不平凡的眼睛。"

读韩偓的诗,我们看到的是一双格外敏锐的眼睛,在季世的暧昧里,捕捉着生命中的每一分诗意与美。

在败德失序的现世,韩偓以精致纯美秀雅端丽的文字,构筑起一个曼妙绝伦的乌托邦。在他对盛唐诗人崔国辅的致敬里,亦有对那个逝去的盛世的缅怀顶礼。

责备他懦弱避世的人们,可曾静心聆听过诗人心底潜流的文化乡愁?

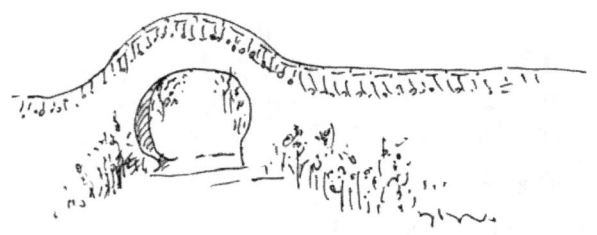

鱼玄机（一首）

江陵愁望有寄

枫叶千枝复万枝，江桥掩映暮帆迟。
忆君心似西江水，日夜东流无歇时。

To—

Along the bridge
myriads of maple leaves
set off each other
Dusk finds some sails return late
My love and thoughts of you
are like the western river
flowing eastward to the sea
Day and night

【诗绎】

枫叶掩映江桥
迟归的帆犁破暮色
江水日夜流向海洋
我的思念流向你

【品读】

天各一方,并不等于分离。

纵然你的帆是在另一个经纬扬起,我的心潮却依旧为你的思念牵引。

回肠九回后,犹自剩回肠。诗中细美幽约的情感、清丽芊绵的意象,像词:

枫叶、江桥、暮帆,忆君心似西江水。东流日夜无歇,掩映迟,千枝复万枝。

《花间集》固然是词的不祧之祖,但在工于感慨的晚唐诗中亦已有了词的因子,这却少有人注意。

杜荀鹤(一首)

送人游吴

君到姑苏见,人家尽枕河。
古宫闲地少,水港小桥多。
夜市卖菱藕,春船载绮罗。
遥知未眠月,乡思在渔歌。

He is Leaving

When you travel in Suzhou
you'll see houses on canals
The Old Palace has no space to spare
Jetties and bridges are seen everywhere
You'll buy caltrops and lotus
at the night market
Silk and satin are transported
by boat in spring
I know you'll stay up in the pale moon
Full of fishermen's
Songs and homesickness

【诗绎】

水港

小桥

人家

古老的宫殿

绵绵的运河

夜市卖莲藕

春船载绮罗

淡淡月光下

悠悠渔歌里

乡思掩上来

未眠的你

如雾

【品读】

整首诗就像一曲恬淡的渔歌,在有月亮的晚上,喃喃地哼唱……

清词丽句必为邻。当晚唐诗人将目光回向六朝时,吸引他们并为他们所着力汲取的并不单纯是意境与辞采,而更是一种物恋的方式与心态。

艺术的回返,总是为了前行。

www.ingramcontent.com/pod-product-compliance
Lightning Source LLC
Chambersburg PA
CBHW070547010526
44118CB00012B/1255